BEAT TEACHER BURNOUT WITH BETTER BOUNDARIES

The Secret to Thriving in Teaching Without Sacrificing Your Personal Life

GRACE STEVENS

Copyright © 2024 by Grace Stevens

Published by Red Lotus Books

Grace Stevens LLC

ISBN: 978-0-9987019-8-1

An abridged version of this book was previously published as *The Ultimate Boundary Playbook for Teachers* in 2023.

All rights reserved.

No part of this book may be reproduced in any form or by any electronic or mechanical means, including information storage and retrieval systems, without written permission from the author, except for the use of brief quotations in a book review.

Disclaimer

This book offers information and is designed for educational purposes only. This information is not a substitute for, nor does it replace professional medical advice, diagnosis, or treatment. The author and publisher shall have neither liability nor responsibility to any person or entity with respect to any loss or damage caused or alleged to be caused directly or indirectly by this book.

Bonus Companion Workbook

To ensure that you receive maximum benefit from this book, please **download the printable Companion Workbook**. For a limited time it is available to you **FREE of charge** at

www.gracestevens.com/boundariesworkbook

It includes full-size PDFs of the worksheets in this book, additional exercises and print and go copies of the boundary scripts.

Prefer to learn by video?

For information on an **on-demand course** that covers material from this book (and so much more!) visit:

www.gracestevens.com/lifeback

Contents

Prologue 1

PART I
Why is Setting Healthy Boundaries So Important? 5

1. Misconceptions & Mindsets 13
2. Boundary Basics - 12 Rules of Engagement 20

PART II
Boundaries at School 25

3. Boundaries on Your Time: Do Less at School 27
4. Saying "No" with Confidence & Professionalism 36
5. Setting Boundaries with Co-Workers 56
6. Setting Boundaries with Parents 75
7. Setting Boundaries with Students 93

PART III
Setting Boundaries with Family and Friends 113

8. Protecting Your Peace Outside of School 115

PART IV
Covert Boundary Issues 131

9. Codependency, Over-Functioning and Oversharing 133

Part V
All the Good Stuff in One Place
Conclusion 143

10. The Scripts All In One Place 145

Part VI
Supplemental Materials
Good Teacher Karma 171
About the Author 173
Also by Grace Stevens 175

Prologue

 "This is why I'm doing it. This is the thing that sets my heart on fire."

-Elizabeth Gilbert, Author

THERE IS A MEME THAT CIRCULATES INSTAGRAM AND FACEBOOK feeds for teachers. It says, "If you've never spent your lunchtime in your car crying, are you even a teacher?" Sad, but also, unfortunately, true.

IN MY PARTICULAR CASE, BEING SOMEONE WHO WALKED TO SCHOOL often, I didn't have the luxury of crying in a car. On several occasions when I did need to be left alone to fall apart, I could be found in a fetal position, under my desk, out of student eyeshot through the windows, hyperventilating and sobbing. I got smarter. I got into the habit of closing the blinds before lunch and had mini-posters with magnets on the back that I could easily use to cover the security window in the door. That solved the problem of being discovered by students peering through the windows. It never got to the root of the problem of why my chosen career created enough anxiety, frustration, and overwhelm to require me to break down regularly in the first place. This was a deeper problem. And one not so easily fixed with magnetic mini-posters.

I MENTION THIS BECAUSE, IF YOU KNOW ME PERSONALLY, YOU MAY be rolling your eyes at the notion that I'm writing a book about setting healthy boundaries. As far as school-life balance went, there were many years that I struggled in this area. My physical, mental, and emotional health, as well as my relationships, suffered because of it. But as with all the healthy habits I teach and write about, setting healthy boundaries is something I studied, applied, practiced, and improved. I fixed it for myself before it occurred to me to help others.

Here's what I learned. If you start with the correct mindset and follow the formula, setting boundaries is a skill anyone can master.

MANY OF US WERE CONDITIONED TO BE PEOPLE PLEASERS AND taught that advocating for our needs was selfish. Relearning those patterns takes work. But doing so is essential if we want to experience the best of life and enjoy healthy relationships. If we want to show up as our best selves for our families, friends, and students.

IF WE DON'T CARE FOR OURSELVES AND OUR ENERGY, WE ARE LITTLE use to anyone else. Learning to set healthy boundaries is an excellent place to start.

So this is what sets my heart on fire: helping teachers craft a more positive experience for themselves and their students.

I used to feel shame that I struggled in certain areas. My natural teaching vibe was modern-day, upbeat Mary Poppins (my British accent helped), and I was known for writing on positive mindset habits. I felt embarrassed to tell people I didn't have it all together.

But one day, it occurred to me that I wouldn't want to take swimming lessons from somebody who had only read about swimming in a book. The person who struggled to swim, almost drowned, and now knew the skill and how to navigate the waters with grace- that's the swimming teacher I wanted.

Over the past few years, I've learned to be more transparent about my struggles with anxiety, depression, and boundaries. They make me human and open to welcoming others who struggle with compassion and without judgment. Less romantically positioned than Liz Gilbert's quote, I feel a little like a teacher equivalent of Andy Dufresne in the Shawshank Redemption, who famously,

"...crawled through a river of sh** and came out clean the other side."

. . .

So let me teach you how to swim. With love and compassion. With practical tips and scripts. Let me be your water wings until you get comfortable in the water.

As an educator, you must learn to set healthy boundaries. If you do not, you will burn out and feel yourself pulled under the water. No one is coming to save you, and no one is going to give you permission to do less. It would be best if you learned to save yourself from drowning.

Everyone, even the most "people pleasing," compliant, conflict-avoidant among us can learn to set healthier boundaries, and I'm excited to teach you how.

PART I

Why is Setting Healthy Boundaries So Important?

Let me ask you this - would you leave the door to your classroom unlocked overnight or even over lunch period? Would you leave the door wide open and invite anyone and everyone in, letting them rifle through your drawers and have complete access to your belongings and your students?

Of course not! In schools, we have physical fences, locks, cameras, and alarms to protect ourselves and our students. We have drills and protocols to keep intruders out, and ourselves safe.

Often, people think of boundaries like fences - something practical that we put up to protect our property, our belongings, and our physical well-being.

. . .

We are skilled and trained in protecting our classroom and our students from physical harm. We are less skilled and intentional at setting boundaries to protect our emotional and mental wellbeing.

That's where this book comes in. It will help you learn the skills and gain the confidence to protect your time, your energy, your mental and emotional health, and, ultimately, avoid burnout in your chosen career in education. Boundaries go beyond just fences: boundaries are about your needs, desires, preferences, and yes, your non-negotiables. Communicating your boundaries is also about teaching people what you find acceptable and how you want to be treated.

Without being intentional about setting boundaries, people can easily infringe on your rights, preferences, and desires. You will feel taken advantage of and resentment grows. Not because your co-workers, administrators, students, or parents are out to get you, but because in education there is a fundamental math problem. The problem is that there are not enough hours in our contracted day to complete all that is required of us. The minutes just don't add up. We can't keep working until our work is "done." Even utilizing all the productivity hacks in the world, all of the tasks never get done.

Additionally, if you've been in education any amount of time you also know this - if you are someone who seems to easily keep up with everything without being overly stressed, you will have more duties and responsibilities handed to you. It's the nature of the beast. Education is always underfunded, and resources are always spread too thin. It's unlikely that your administrator has a personal vendetta against you, they are likely overburdening you out of convenience to them. If you are known to agree to additional duties without too much drama, you are simply an easy target when something extra gets put on their plate. It's on us to get out of victim mode and get into empowerment mode. It's on us to learn how to set boundaries, communicate these boundaries, and hold ourselves and others accountable to them.

Now all of that can sound very scary and against our nature as "helpers." But if you stick with me, you will learn that setting and communicating healthy boundaries is actually a very loving thing to do.

Many of us have maladaptive communication styles. We have been conditioned to be polite and helpful. We say "yes" to things we want to say "no" to, and we say we don't mind when actually we do. This lack of candor is the breeding ground for resentment and is intrinsically unfair to the people we love. People shouldn't be expected to read our minds.

Learning to set and communicate healthy boundaries is a foundational skill many of us are lacking. And whether being taken advantage of is real or perceived, feelings of resentment and burnout quickly grow. This can be very damaging not only to our teaching experience but to our emotional health and all of our relationships.

. . .

But I promise you it is possible to learn how to set healthy boundaries, and I guarantee there are people on your campus who have figured this out. Do you know how to spot them?

They are the teachers who seem less stressed than everyone else. They are rarely or never the last car on campus. They are not caught battling with the vending machine for a 2 PM pick-me-up from a highly caffeinated drink. They remain calm despite the unrealistic demands of students' parents. They are having a more positive experience of teaching or being an administrator than you are.

Have you ever wondered what their secret is? Are they smarter than you? Do they magically get all the "easy" students and low-maintenance parents on their roster? Probably not. The only difference between you and them is that they are more practiced and more consistent in setting and maintaining healthy boundaries.

Here's my simple commitment to you. In this book, I will eliminate all the fluff and provide you with simple, sustainable strategies. You will find instructions on where and how to set boundaries and sample scripts to get you started until you gain more confidence.

Please don't assume that the length of this book is any reflection of its value. It is short by design. No educator I know has time to dig through pages of research and stories. We all know the professional development that took all day but could have been delivered in an hour, and I avoid that at all costs. This playbook is designed to teach you strategies, give you confidence, and provide you with scripts to start setting better boundaries as soon as tomorrow because you can read this entire book today.

Downloading the Companion Workbook and working through the exercises will give you a deeper experience, but even those exercises are designed to be short, impactful, and geared towards immediate results. Be sure to grab the workbook so you can experience everything this book has to offer. The information on how to access it is at the beginning of the book.

Who is this book for?

You are in the right place if any of the following resonate with you:

• You are employed in education - as a teacher, administrator, curriculum coach, teaching aide, special education or speech pathologist, or school counselor. Heck, even if you drive the school bus or supervise the schoolyard.

• You want to leave campus at a reasonable time each day without dragging home a cart full of work or a heart full of teacher guilt.

• You are frustrated that you are easily coerced into taking on extra duties and roles that do not interest you and that fall outside your contractual obligations.

- You feel the pressure to accommodate parent, co-worker, and even student requests despite knowing they are unreasonable and beyond your scope of duty.

- You are on the fast road to burnout and want to better separate school from home.

- Your family and other people complain about how much of your life is consumed by school.

- You love education but want time and energy for other things you love, too.

- You're tired of being "teacher tired" and worry that continuing at this pace will be unsustainable.

- You know you need to set better boundaries, but you need more confidence in how to do so in an effective, loving, and stress-free way that can improve every aspect of your life.

You will also find this book helpful if any of these ideas resonate in **your personal life**:

- You struggle to effectively communicate your preferences and desires and assume that it should be obvious to your partner or family what you want.

- You find yourself saying "I don't mind" to suggestions when you do mind.

- You reluctantly agree to things your family wants to do because you don't want to appear high maintenance or inflexible or (especially if it's with regards to something your parents want) ungrateful.

- You find yourself agreeing to things to maintain harmony and avoid drama, or you have taken on the self-appointed role of peacekeeper.

If any of this sounds like it could apply to you, **you are not alone.** Please know that. Lacking confidence in setting healthy boundaries is not a character defect. It's just something we have never been taught. And let's be honest, we work in an education system that has a "self-sacrifice" culture (more on that later) that thrives and takes advantages of that fact.

1

Misconceptions & Mindsets

Let's start by debunking some misconceptions that you might have around setting boundaries.

MISCONCEPTION #1

I can't change other people's behavior.

A common misconception is that boundaries are about other people's behavior. You may feel that people in your life would not be receptive to you suddenly setting boundaries.

 Setting boundaries is about *your* behavior, not other people's behavior.

It's about deciding and communicating what is acceptable to *you* and how *you* will behave. You get to decide what is preferable and non-negotiable, what you will tolerate, and what you will not. Setting boundaries is about how you act and prioritize your needs and desires.

. . .

MISCONCEPTION #2

People who set boundaries are aggressive and inflexible.

You may be aware of the adage that says, "you teach people how to treat you by what you tolerate." If you do not set and enforce your boundaries, people may not know how to treat you. This isn't their fault. Few people are mind readers. If you do not tell others your boundaries, they will not be able to respect them. Therefore, it is your responsibility to set, communicate, and enforce your limitations. You can do so in a way that is loving and clear. No one needs to be aggressive about it.

Knowing and respecting people's boundaries is the foundation of a healthy relationship. They are integral to successful relationships in every area of your life and essential to true self-care. By setting and communicating boundaries correctly, you invest in yourself and your relationships. That is loving behavior, the opposite of being aggressive.

MISCONCEPTION #3

Setting boundaries is difficult.

Maybe you are uncomfortable setting boundaries simply because you don't know how. This will be especially true if you haven't had healthy role models in this area. You may be the type of person that naturally feels uncomfortable with conflict and avoids it.

To overcome the misperception that setting boundaries is difficult, you must adopt a growth mindset. You can learn hard things. You just aren't comfortable communicating and enforcing your boundaries *yet*. It's a skill that you can learn like any other.

Will you have to stretch yourself out of your comfort zone at first? Yes. Will it be worth it? Absolutely.

MISCONCEPTION #4

Setting boundaries will upset people

As mentioned before, people can't read minds. When setting and communicating boundaries in a positive, professional and loving way, setting boundaries strengthens relationships. This is true in both professional and personal relationships.

Whenever you set a boundary, you and the other party involved become aware of what is expected of each other. As a result, the relationship's expectations become realistic and come with clear directions. Typically, people behave correctly when they know what is expected of them. So, setting boundaries and providing clear directions creates realistic expectations that all parties can respect.

Some people will be surprised if you suddenly start setting boundaries where there were none before.

Here are some likely examples:

- Your co-worker who expects you to do the lion's share of the lesson planning or who is very comfortable with you always to pick up the extra duties.
- The administrator who can always rely on you to show up to all the extra meetings, committees, school dances, and sporting events.
- Maybe even the friend who assumes you'll pick up the check or your spouse who takes for granted that you will pick up the kids, the house, and the groceries.

The list goes on. If reading the above makes you uncomfortable and you find yourself nodding and feeling resentment, then it's even more important that you commit to the strategies in this book and level up your boundary-setting game.

Cue Some "Real Talk" and Tough Love

Here's some tough love for you. The people who will become prickly when you start setting boundaries are the people who have benefitted from you not having them previously. They could be benefitting consciously or unconsciously. I'm not painting anyone as an evil villain. It's natural for people to fall into specific roles and habits in their professional and personal relationships.

If you were drawn to this book, it is because somewhere inside, you recognize a fundamental inequity in these roles and responsibilities, and you need to make some positive changes. It would be best if you were proactive in setting new rules to protect your time, energy, and peace, and getting comfortable setting healthy boundaries is the answer.

Sure, people in your life who care about you may act a little surprised at first. But ultimately, they will champion you for advocating for yourself and your needs. People who continue to push back and resist your efforts to make positive changes in your life aren't your people. If they are in your family, that's going to be tough. Ultimately, you may have to limit your exposure to them. If they are at your school, that's easier. While having productive, friendly, and equitable working relationships with our administrators and colleagues is always ideal, it should never be a popularity contest. It's okay for people to work, collaborate, and plan with you effectively without being your friend. You should never feel you must compromise your boundaries to put other people's comfort before your own.

BRENE BROWN SUMS IT UP BEST:

> "Daring to set boundaries is about having the courage to love ourselves, even when we risk disappointing others."

An Inconvenient Truth - Educators Are Not Great at Setting Boundaries

I'm going to make a sweeping generalization. While there may be a few outliers to my anecdotal observation, it is based on having worked in education for over two decades. And it's this: as a general rule, teachers tend to be conflict avoidant and often prefer to accommodate requests than seem inflexible by saying "no." Am I right?

Here are some potential reasons for this.

First, teaching is a helping profession that attracts people who want to impact others positively. Note that "helping" should not be synonymous with "people pleasing." But generally, we want to go the extra mile to accommodate people because it's more comfortable to our nature than to stand up for ourselves and confront others.

Next, we've bought into the collective narrative that teaching is a "calling." We have been conditioned to see teaching as more than just a job, more than just a means to procure a paycheck. And for most educators, teaching is so much more. We are not just looking to make money, we want to make an impact. They are looking to change lives and influence the future. Because let's face it, there are plenty of ways to make more money working fewer hours and with less education (and less student loans).

 However, the dark side of this narrative is that educators can find themselves manipulated and guilt-tripped into working too many hours, being way too accommodating to ridiculous requests, and burning themselves out emotionally and physically

because everything is (you know what's coming) " for the kids." We've watched too many Hollywood movies that celebrate teachers as superheroes when we are in fact very human. We have physical needs such as rest, anxiety-free sleep, and time to take care of our bodies and health, not to mention many other life responsibilities.

Here's a scenario many educators can relate to - the guilt we feel at being short-tempered, distracted, and impatient at home with our own children because we have spent all of our emotional and physical energy taking care of other people's children.

Often, the people in our lives who deserve the best of us rarely get it. And as for authentic self-care, we simply don't have time to make it a priority.

Finally, many educators have bought into the collective (yet false) narrative that correlates time spent on campus to effectiveness as a teacher and dedication to students. The idea is that the teacher who works the most is the better teacher. Teachers who consistently leave campus on time are secretly judged as not being as committed to student success.

Are there some lazy teachers out there who are tenured and rely on protection from their teachers union to hide their inadequacies? Probably. But they are a tiny minority. Most teachers want the best for their students and work hard to achieve this daily.

Some educators have found a way to set appropriate boundaries, manage their time effectively, and prioritize having balance in their lives so that they can come to school energized and bring the best of themselves to their students every day. Good for them! We need to stop judging and shaming them for it.

So yes, educators in general are not good at setting boundaries. We need to change that.

Let's get started!

2

Boundary Basics - 12 Rules of Engagement

Before we jump into specific scenarios and strategies, let's get clear on some basic rules of engagement when setting boundaries.

1. FIX YOUR MINDSET

Understand that you have a right to set boundaries. As we discussed, letting people know your expectations and limits is respectful and the foundation of healthy relationships, professionally and personally.

2. REMEMBER YOUR BOUNDARY RIGHTS

• You have a right to say "no" without guilt.

• You have a right to be treated respectfully.

• You have a right to put your needs on par with someone else's.

- You have a right to reject other people's unreasonable expectations.

3. Use "I" language

Remember, boundaries are about YOUR behavior; they are not about controlling other people. When discussing them, use sentences that begin with "I" and not "you," which can put people on the defensive and make them feel attacked. For example, saying, "I feel overwhelmed when..." instead of "You make me feel overwhelmed when you..." takes the blame off the other person and is more likely to result in positive outcomes.

We will look at sample scripts in detail later, but for now, remember this rule of engagement - "I" statements.

4. Remember, you are not the only person in this conversation

The other person will have needs, preferences, and boundaries too. Actively listen and approach the discussion with a "win-win" mentality. That is to say, approach the conversation with the goal of both parties getting their needs met.

5. Consider the timing and the location of the discussion

In general, personal relationship boundaries should be talked about in private. Even if the person is a co-worker, you may not want to confront or embarrass them in front of other colleagues. Other times, you may want a witness to your conversation. This may be appropriate if someone repeatedly ignores your boundaries or tries to bully you into taking on extra responsibilities or duties that you have politely and repeatedly declined. In this case, schedule a meeting with someone and let them know you are bringing a neutral party along to help facilitate the discussion and take notes.

6. No surprise conversations

Whether discussing boundaries in private or public, plan ahead and set up a meeting. Even a casual "When's a good time to talk to you about something today?" is better than interrupting someone when they are working or talking to someone else. This is more respectful and allows you to gather your thoughts to approach the conversation in the most gentle and productive way.

7. Know the difference between preferences, desires, and non-negotiables

Preferences and desires can be flexible. Non-negotiables should be just that - not up for negotiation. Non-negotiables include anything you feel is dangerous, unethical, or goes against your core values.

8. Don't take resistance personally

Be prepared that people might need time to adjust their expectations, especially if they are not used to you stating your preferences and boundaries.

. . .

9. BE PREPARED TO ENFORCE A CONSEQUENCE IF IT'S A NON-negotiable

Remember, setting boundaries isn't about controlling or punishing others. The consequence will be about what you follow through on - and that may ultimately be stepping away from the situation or relationship.

10. TAKE THE "HIGH ROAD"

If people become hostile, agitated, or unethical, rise above and don't compromise your values or lower your communication styles to their level. Whenever possible and preferable, maintain confidentiality. Don't add fuel to the fire by gossiping about the interaction. If the issue is a matter of ethical concern and you need to escalate it to your superiors, do so confidentially and professionally. You will never regret taking the high road.

11. PLAN AND PRACTICE WHAT YOU WILL SAY BEFORE YOU APPROACH your conversation

This not only gives you confidence but allows you to phrase things in a kind way - *the goal is for people to understand that you are rejecting their proposition, not that you are rejecting them.*

12. START SLOW

Don't tackle your most frustrating or stressful boundary issue right out of the gate. Start with some low-stakes preferences to gain your confidence and find your authentic voice in boundary setting. While the scripts I provide are an excellent start, over time you should gain confidence and find your style and vocabulary for setting boundaries in a way that feels natural to you.

Getting boundaries is not always a "yes/no" proposition. An excellent place to start flexing your boundary muscle is to set boundaries with limits. If it's tough for you to start with a "no" to a request, give a "yes" with strict limits– and then stick to them.

PART II

Boundaries at School

3

Boundaries on Your Time: Do Less at School

So I'll state the obvious - educators, you do too much. Also, in the spirit of tough love (and because it was my experience for twenty years), no one is ever going to explicitly give you permission to do less.

CAN TEACHERS AND ADMINISTRATORS COMPLETE ALL OF THEIR required tasks within contract hours? Probably not consistently. The latest research from Edweek.org (https://www.edweek.org/teaching-learning/heres-how-many-hours-a-week-teachers-work/) estimated that in 2019 the average teacher worked between 15-20 hours per week beyond their contract hours. That means the average teacher donated thirteen and a half 40-hour weeks to the education system. That is insane! So even if you feel skipping out of campus every day as soon as the bell rings (or whatever your contract dictates) is unrealistic, there is still a lot of improvement every single one of us can make.

. . .

AGAIN, THIS DATA WAS FROM 2019. NO ONE IN EDUCATION HAS been working fewer hours since the pandemic, so the average teacher working 55 hours a week is likely a low estimate.

HERE'S WHAT I KNOW FOR SURE. YOU WILL ALWAYS HAVE MORE TO do than you can complete within your contract hours. To work fewer hours and achieve a better school-life balance, you must do the following:

1 DEVELOP NINJA TIME MANAGEMENT SKILLS.

2 Start advocating for yourself (and your students).

3 Get fiercely protective of your planning period or prep time.

4 Get comfortable with declining requests that fall beyond the scope of your contract.

5 Set boundaries with pushy parent and student requests.

AN IN-DEPTH ANALYSIS OF ITEM ONE ON THE LIST IS BEYOND THE scope of this book, although I will give you some "quick hit" ideas and frameworks. Achieving items 2 - 5 on this list is the focus of this book and where the magic happens.

IN THIS SECTION, I WILL GIVE YOU SOME QUICK STRATEGIES TO help you prioritize and ultimately eliminate tasks. I will also reveal the secret to declining requests professionally and confidently. If you ever feel awkward and pressured to take on committees, meetings, and additional duties that you are not interested in, this "secret" may be the piece you were missing. I can't wait for you to learn it and get comfortable implementing it.

Doing Less

I said that time management and productivity skills were beyond the scope of this book, and I promised you a down-and-dirty, no-fluff guide to setting boundaries. However, there are a couple of productivity tools that can quickly help you with setting boundaries.

FIRST, LET'S ELIMINATE SOME TASKS. RECOGNIZE THAT THERE IS more on your list on any given day than you can finish. The only way to feel that you are making an impact without "living at school" is to finish some tasks quicker, and to eliminate others altogether.

IN MY ONLINE COURSES, I COACH TEACHERS ON HOW TO SET UP A teaching North Star - a compass to guide them when setting priorities. It's a well-thought-out vision for what is most important to them and a helpful tool when helping them evaluate what on their to-do list they are going to intentionally drop as low priority.

Spoiler alert; most teachers' North Star points towards student success. That's why we signed up for the job.

Following this compass makes it easy to determine which of your long lists of tasks actually have to do with other people's agendas and bookkeeping responsibilities, and nothing to do with actual student success.

One example could be endless data reports where by the time all of the data gets aggregated on someone else's spreadsheet it is already out of date and not pertinent to drive instruction. Am I saying don't complete data reports for your supervisor? No. I'm saying they *may* fall under low-priority tasks and you should spend as little time on them as possible. Honestly, does compiling endless data reports ever tell you anything *you* don't already know about where students are struggling? Sometimes you just have to scratch things off your list, knowing that if they are truly important someone will send you a second email about them. In my experience, at least 50% of the time the second request doesn't come. People either forget or just figure out a different way to get their answer or information they need.

A HELPFUL TOOL TO HELP WITH STREAMLINING YOUR TO-DO LIST IS a decision matrix (sometimes called an Eisenhower Matrix).

A decision matrix is a tool that helps you quickly identify which tasks you need to prioritize, which you can delay, and which you can delete. There is a section for delegating.

AS TEACHERS, WE FEEL WE HAVE NO ONE TO WHOM WE CAN delegate. Few teachers have aides or administrative support people to help them. But don't underestimate how many tasks you can delegate to students and parent volunteers. Parent volunteers are more common in the elementary school setting, but middle school and high school teachers may have student TAs (teaching aides) available to them, so there should be someone who can take a few tasks off your plate.

What kind of tasks can you delegate?

. . .

First, consider the many tasks you perform each day that could become part of a classroom routine. Come up with ways to streamline procedures.

For example, collecting and organizing papers. Maintaining an organized class library. Some processes for distributing and ordering supplies. A system for doing attendance and lunch count that doesn't involve you calling each student by name.

What about grading? Can you implement routines and processes, such as peer grading quizzes or simple (non-subjective) things such as spelling tests or math homework?

Make a list of all the daily repetitive tasks in your classroom, and see if they can be systematized. It takes time to set up systems and have students practice them, but it's a good investment of time. Ask colleagues or other teachers you follow on social media for suggestions and look on Pinterest or YouTube for examples. Even if you can save yourself 10 minutes a day, that would amount to an extra hour a week that you could put to excellent use. Over a school year, that would give you back 36 hours.

What could you delegate to a parent or a TA? TAs are excellent for inputting grades and sorting papers. Your district may have student confidentiality rules that disqualify parent volunteers from viewing or inputting grades. However, there are still many extra activities that you take on as a teacher that you could delegate to them. Here are just a few ways I have used parent helpers in the past:

- THE COORDINATION AND RUNNING OF CLASS PARTIES

- Researching potential educational field trips - including emailing prospective places for group rates and availability and researching transportation

- The coordination of a reading incentive program for students; tracking their reading points (easily accomplished if you have an Accelerated Reader program or similar), procuring and distributing rewards and certificates

- Helping set up field day or student activity day

- Helping plan, fundraise, and decorate for 8th-grade promotion and high school graduation

THESE ARE JUST A FEW EXAMPLES OF THINGS I HAVE DONE. Network with colleagues or online groups to see how to utilize student and parent help to reduce your tasks.

DOES THE IDEA OF HANDING OFF ANY OF THESE TASKS CAUSE YOU stress? sk yourself if your reluctance to delegate any of these items is due to your belief that you are the only person who can effectively complete these tasks. This may be a clue that you are buying into the "teacher martyr" myth or that you have boundary issues with over-functioning. Simply put, over-functioning is when you consistently do more than is necessary, appropriate, or healthy. I'll address this more in the bonus section "Covert Boundary Issues."

. . .

LEVERAGE TECHNOLOGY

FOR MANY EDUCATORS, ARTIFICIAL INTELLIGENCE SITES SUCH AS ChatGPT have become as frustrating and invasive in their classroom as fidget spinners and the bottle flip challenge. Unlike the latter two fads, AI is not going to fizzle out.

I FIND EDUCATORS GENERALLY FALL INTO TWO CAMPS. CAMP ONE includes teachers who stress over AI and feel that monitoring student work for AI-generated content is just one more burden put on them. Camp two includes the teachers who recognize what an amazing time-saving tool AI can be to streamline and automate many of their tasks. Please let me invite you to camp two.

I AM NOT AN AI EXPERT, BUT HERE IS A LIST OF JUST A FEW TASKS that AI can help any teacher with. Again, many wonderful educators have YouTube and TikTok videos and resources to show you in detail how to do these things, and many more. By the time you read this book, it is likely that AI will have even more amazing features, but for now, I just want to open your mind to the possibilities and opportunities for saving time that some of these tools offer.

HERE ARE SOME TASKS AI COULD HELP YOU WITH:

. . .

AI can create parent letters, emails, and other communication documents for you in a fraction of the time it would take you to write them from scratch.

Translating letters and real-time communication with parents who don't read or speak English.

Translating course materials - AI can instantly translate instructional materials into multiple languages to support ESL students.

Recording and transcribing lectures - AI speech recognition can automate transcription and note-taking during lectures for students who missed class.

Using the transcript, AI can also produce lecture summaries and study notes & study guides.

Research for lesson and unit planning. AI assistants can rapidly search databases and materials to identify relevant readings, activities, discussion prompts, and multimedia resources tailored to lesson objectives.

Differentiated instruction. AI can summarize complex writing pieces and in addition to analyzing for main ideas, key details, and structure, it can produce several versions to support students at different reading levels.

. . .

CREATE LESSON PLAN TEMPLATES. BASED ON GRADE LEVEL, SUBJECT matter, and learning goals, AI can pull customizable lesson plan templates for teachers to populate.

HELPING YOU COME UP WITH IDEAS. FOR EXAMPLE, A SIMPLE prompt such as "Give me 36 inspirational quotes for high schoolers around the subject of XYZ" could help you plan out an entire year of homeroom weekly meeting slides. Bonus points, ask AI to put them in a spreadsheet, head over to something like Canva (an easy graphics program - free for educators), select a template, and import the quotes and it will make all the slides for you.

HONESTLY, THE POSSIBILITIES ARE ENDLESS. A QUICK GOOGLE search can help you come up with so many more ways educators are using AI to give them back hours in their week.

OK, BEYOND ALL THE DELEGATING AND STREAMLINING, IF YOU want to truly avoid burnout and protect your time and energy, you are going to have to get comfortable declining requests for extra duties and taking on additional responsibilities. That's what we will tackle together in the next section.

4

Saying "No" with Confidence & Professionalism

In this section, I will give you three tools that will immediately help you gain clarity and confidence in setting boundaries on your time.

First, we will look at mindset. Why is "no" such a powerful word?

Then, you will complete a quick inventory of all the adjunct (fancy word for extra and unpaid) duties that you are currently committed to.

Finally, you will learn the "Anatomy of a No" framework you can return to whenever you need to effectively and professionally decline requests.

The power of "no"

Let's start with mindset. In the Supplemental Materials section, I have included a worksheet titled "Yes/No" framework. Full-size PDFs that you can make copies of are available in the downloadable Companion Workbook. Again, the information on how to access the workbook is at the beginning of this book.

THE "YES/NO" FRAMEWORK IS A TOOL THAT CAN REMIND YOU OF the "why" behind your "nos." The idea here is to remind you that every time you say "yes" to something, you are saying "no" to something else. It's a tool to help you evaluate, "What does that "yes" really cost me?"

FOR EXAMPLE, WHENEVER I SAY YES TO AN EXTRACURRICULAR activity, I say no to time with my family, my hobbies, or other school projects that I am more passionate about. You get the idea.

EVERY TIME I POLITELY SAY "NO" TO THAT CO-WORKER WHO COMES into my room during my prep period and starts talking to me, so I end up completing nothing I'd planned, I am saying "yes" to respecting my boundaries and time.

SO THAT'S THE MINDSET PIECE. EVERY YES COSTS YOU SOMETHING, just as every no cost you something. Only you can weigh the costs.

THE POWER OF "YES" WITH LIMITATIONS

Remember, there may be situations where you have a limited "yes." So you agree to something but with reasonable limitations. This can be a good place to get some practice setting boundaries until you gain more confidence. Think of it like floaty wings in the water. Again, it's best not to start with high-stakes issues– get some practice first.

Here are some examples:

School event supervision: "I can help supervising the science fair next Wednesday, but I'll need to leave by 6pm to catch my son's soccer practice."

Committee involvement: "I can serve on the curriculum committee again this year, as long as meetings are scheduled during my planning periods so I don't have to stay after school."

Academic coaching: "I'm happy to help coach the math team this semester, but I won't be available for competitions or events outside of our regular Wednesday meeting time from 3-4pm."

Peer mentoring: "I'm willing to mentor a new teacher, as long as we limit meetings to 30 minutes per week during my prep period on Thursdays."

Take inventory of your current extra duties

Next, take a moment to complete the "Inventory of Extra Duties" in the Supplemental Material. List all of your current commitments and reflect on how much joy and fulfillment they give you or how much stress and resentment they cause.

Most school districts will have a policy regarding how many hours of adjunct duties you must volunteer for. Given this, choose assignments you enjoy and fill you up rather than activities that drain you.

For example, I will always prefer activities that directly involve students. These include drama club, Science Olympiad, astronomy night, and one-on-one tutoring. I'm not really into athletics but if I were, coaching a sport and cheering students on, that would be awesome duty.

Other teachers may not feel the same way. I once had a teammate who said they could not stand to spend one more minute with students at the end of the day. Their preference was always to volunteer for curriculum committees, writing committees, safety committees, or anything that did not involve students but involved adults sitting around a table or, more recently, sitting on Zoom. Sitting in on a Zoom isn't always a bad thing, as you can have other tabs open on your device and input grades or do other mindless administrative tasks. But overall, to me, all those committees where we "unpack the standards" or sift through data are equivalent to Dante's 9th circle of Purgatory - get me out of there! Different strokes for different folks.

As Simon Sinek says,

"Working hard for something we don't care about is called stress. Working hard for something we love is called passion."

FORTUNATELY, I HAVE A LOT OF PASSION FOR WORKING DIRECTLY with students.

ONLY YOU KNOW WHAT LIGHTS YOU UP AND WHAT DRAINS YOU, SO be strategic when accepting requests to participate in extra duties. Ideally, you have an element of choice, and you can stay in your passion zone.

USE THE INVENTORY FORM TO HELP YOU. AGAIN, FULL-SIZE PDFs are available in the workbook. The inventory form includes several criteria to help you evaluate your extra duties, such as if it provides a stipend, how long the commitment lasts, and if it interests you. Once you start listing them out, you might be surprised (or disappointed) to realize how many additional duties you have taken on or have been assigned.

WHAT ABOUT WHEN YOU ARE APPROACHED WITH A REQUEST THAT IS reasonable, but not within your passion zone?

BE PREPARED TO DECLINE WITH A PROVEN SCRIPT.

YOU MAY BE AWARE OF THIS QUOTE BY THE NOVELIST ANNE Lamotte:

 "No is a complete sentence."

Beat Teacher Burnout with Better Boundaries

THIS QUOTE IS OFTEN FEATURED IN MEMES AND INTENDED TO remind us that we don't owe anybody an apology or a reason for declining their request.

NOW, THAT MIGHT BE TRUE ABOUT SOCIAL INTERACTIONS. BUT IN an educational setting where you are being requested to do something related to your actual job ("related" but not technically part of), you will need to have a little more finesse.

I WILL OUTLINE THE FIVE-STEP PROCESS HERE, INCLUDING THE missing piece that has possibly stopped you from having confidence in declining requests in the past, especially if they are coming from your administrator. Now, you don't need to remember this whole script- you only need to remember the first step. I suggest printing out the 5-step framework from the Companion Workbook and slipping it inside your teacher planner for easy reference.

THE FIRST STEP IS TO BUY YOURSELF SOME TIME BECAUSE HERE'S the reality of how these situations usually happen.

LET'S SAY IT'S A RANDOM DAY, AND YOU'RE LIVING YOUR BEST teacher life. You've probably been on yard duty; you're rushing back to class with full hands, juggling your keys, the copies you just made, your water bottle, and your mug of reheated coffee. Your administrator or a high-profile parent suddenly appears. You are taken by surprise, and beware - they will probably start with a compliment. They'll tell you that you are the perfect person for this job. Of course, you are! You're an ideal candidate because you're a dedicated, people-pleasing sucker who will say yes.

"I'm so glad I ran into you! We have this opportunity. You'll be perfect for it. It's the curriculum/safety/data committee. Oh, it'll only be one meeting a month."

And so it begins.

You are taken by surprise, and you're probably going to be flustered because of all of the things you are balancing in your hand, in addition to the fact that you didn't have time to go to the restroom and your students are waiting outside your door, so you are aware that the potential for an unsupervised riot is looming. If you are flustered and in a hurry, the requestor probably thinks you will just say yes. Don't be the sucker. Buy yourself some time.

It can be as simple as this:

"Hey, thanks for thinking of me. Let me check my schedule and get back to you."

Or as controlled as this:

. . .

"I HAVE A POLICY: I DON'T TAKE ON ANY NEW COMMITMENTS without a 24-hour consideration period. Can you get me more details while I check my schedule and think about it?"

THAT'S ALL YOU HAVE TO REMEMBER. BUY YOURSELF SOME TIME.

NEXT, RESPOND IN WRITING. THIS AVOIDS THE AWKWARDNESS OF saying "no" to someone's face if you find that uncomfortable or fear that you will cave because you'd rather sit in boring meetings for the rest of the year than stand in a moment of discomfort. (I'm not judging you, I'm sympathizing because that used to be my default mode, too.) Additionally, if you respond in writing, you will have a paper trail that you may need to rely on at some point in the future.

WHEN YOU RESPOND IN WRITING, HERE IS THE FORMULA:

1 THANK THEM FOR THINKING OF YOU.

2 Decline. "I am unable to participate in the committee/event this year." Note - do not apologize. Just state the fact. You are unable or choose not to participate or accept the request. There is no need to use the word "sorry." You can take a leaf from our friends at the Apple Genius counter. They are trained not to say, "No, your device is not covered," but to use the words, "As it turns out."

Example: "As it turns out, you are eligible for a device upgrade." See how ninja that is?

. . .

3 GIVE A STUDENT-CENTERED REASON FOR DECLINING. That's the secret sauce right there. Don't tell people the request doesn't fall within your interest or your contractual duties; tell people that you can't participate because your primary concern and responsibility is your students' success. There's no way anyone can object to that.

Here are some examples of student-centered reasons:

"AS YOU MAY BE AWARE, THIS IS MY FIRST YEAR IN THIS PARTICULAR grade assignment. I feel I owe it to my students to spend any additional time I have gaining a firmer grasp of the required curriculum so that I can best support their academic success."

"THIS YEAR, I FIND MYSELF IN A CHALLENGING SITUATION WHERE many of my students struggle with the skills they need to succeed in this grade. I will be dedicating any extra time I have to developing and implementing interventions that help remediate their academic deficiencies." (Note - extra credit if you can get as many educational buzzwords into your reason for declining).

"AS YOU MAY REMEMBER, WE HAD A LOT OF TURNOVER IN THIS grade span this year, and I am now the senior member of the team. I am obliged to devote much of my extracurricular time to training the new teachers on specific lesson planning, data collection, assessments, and interventions that we use. I feel this area of responsibility should be my main focus to ensure the success of all students in this grade."

. . .

YOU GET THE IDEA. MAKE IT ABOUT THE STUDENTS.

4. OFFER ALTERNATIVE SOLUTIONS IF THERE ARE ANY.

5. Wish the person the best of luck with their endeavor.

HERE'S A COMPLETE SAMPLE SCRIPT:

DEAR PRINCIPAL:

Thank you for your invitation to represent our school at the district-wide curriculum committee.

As it turns out, I am unable to participate this year.

You may remember that....*(student-centered reason)*

I am confident that many other qualified staff members can effectively represent our school and ensure that the committee is successful.

Respectfully,

[name]

AGAIN, ALL YOU NEED TO WORRY ABOUT IS REMEMBERING STEP ONE - wait to respond, and buy yourself some time. Then use the sample scripts in this guide to help craft your polite, firm, and professional response.

. . .

WHAT IF YOU ARE NOT READING THIS BOOK AT THE BEGINNING OF the year?

SOME TEACHERS HAVE TOLD ME THAT THEY ARE ALREADY committed to some additional responsibilities this year and feel they need to wait until next year to use this script to decline. This is not necessarily true. You do not want to abandon a duty mid-year without anyone to take up the reins. That would reflect poorly on you unless you had a very good reason (family or health emergency for example). But it doesn't mean you can't approach your administrator mid-year with a request to be relieved of or replaced on your duty. Remember our four magic words, "As in turns out?" Here are some other magic phrases,

"I'VE CHANGED MY MIND."

"My circumstances have changed."

"I'm confident someone else would be interested in this duty."

LET'S ADDRESS ONE MORE SCENARIO, AND THAT'S WHEN IT IS automatically assumed you will take on a specific duty because you have traditionally done it. For example, I worked at one school where one teacher had been solely responsible for putting together the yearbook for about 20 years. You read that correctly. She wasn't even the teacher of the graduating students. Year after year, people just assumed she'd do it. I do believe she didn't mind doing it, but it wasn't exactly a passion project for her. I remember our administrator stressing that if something happened to her we would be left in a bind. No one else had any idea what was involved in putting the yearbook together.

. . .

FOR SIXTEEN YEARS, I WAS RESPONSIBLE FOR RUNNING A DIGITAL Starlab and astronomy night for my school. It was a ton of work and involved me picking up the equipment (a 40-mile drive roundtrip), loading it up (it took up a whole van), setting it up at school, lesson planning for a sub for an entire week to be with my class, and lesson planning the astronomy curriculum for all nine grades that I worked with in the Starlab. Oh, and I had to go on a Saturday every other year to get recertified to handle the equipment. What was the stipend? Zero. Why did I continue to do it? Because it was my favorite week of school! I got to build relationships with every student on campus and watch them grow every year as they came through Starlab.

AT ONE POINT, THERE WAS ANOTHER STAFF MEMBER WHO GOT trained with me. This was lucky because one year, at 9 PM the night before Starlab week, I had an emergency appendectomy. In fact, when I came around from surgery a nurse asked me, "What's Starlab?" Apparently, I had been babbling that I had to get to school to "do Starlab" right up until the moment they put me under anesthesia. So yeah, I wasn't exactly the poster child for setting healthy boundaries at that point in my career. I have an even worse story of how stubborn I was about needing to be at school when I was dangerously ill. Honestly, I'm too embarrassed to share it here. Maybe one day it will slip out on my podcast. But you get the point, zero boundaries.

ANYWAY, STARLAB CAME AND WENT WITHOUT ME. THE OTHER teacher pulled it off. And after I left the school another teacher went and got trained. And negotiated a stipend! :)

. . .

HERE'S THE POINT OF THIS ANECDOTE. DON'T LET YOURSELF BE fooled or guilted into doing things that go beyond the scope of your responsibilities solely because an administrator has you convinced that "If you don't do it, no one will and the students will miss out."

I'M CALLING BS (BOUNDARY SHAM) ON THAT.

IN MY PREVIOUS EXAMPLE, LET'S SAY THAT MY ROCKSTAR colleague who was in charge of the yearbook suddenly quit, or had to leave midyear. I love her, so let's imagine some lovely scenario where she won the lottery and decided not to finish out the year. Do you really think the students wouldn't have had a yearbook? Another teacher, a parent, or someone else would have stepped up. A quick phone call to another school for help, watching some YouTube videos, calling the publisher of the yearbook. All of these would result in someone getting up to speed with the task pretty quickly.

AS MY DEAR FATHER TOLD ME MANY TIMES,

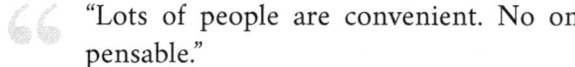

> "Lots of people are convenient. No one is indispensable."

People will figure it out. Educators are amazingly resourceful.

There is an exception to all of the above. And that is when the duty is something attached to your grade span or department.

Examples would include:

- Coordinating and going to science camp with your students if you are the science teacher
- Organizing promotion/graduation if your students are in the graduating class (for example, 8th grade promotion)
- Science Olympiad or putting on the science fair if you are the science teacher
- Math club/competitions if you are the math teacher
- Coordinating and supervising concerts and performances if you are the music teacher

IN THESE CIRCUMSTANCES, IT IS REASONABLE TO ASSUME THAT A particular teacher takes on the duty. Most teachers would have considered this before agreeing to the grade assignment. But in certain circumstances, you might want to opt-out for a year.

LET'S SAY YOU HAVE YOUR OWN CHILD GRADUATING A PARTICULAR year and you want to volunteer for their graduation festivities at their school. This would be an issue not just because you have limited time, but because both events could be happening on the same day. Or your child is involved in a sport and dates conflict with athletic competition dates. Maybe you want to go to the county spelling bee or science fair as a parent, not a judge.

HERE ARE SOME SUGGESTIONS TO HELP NAVIGATE THESE SITUATIONS most positively. This situation warrants more finesse than, "I've changed my mind."

1. GIVE YOUR ADMINISTRATOR AND CO-TEACHERS AS MUCH warning as possible. Ideally, plant the seed of "I'm not going to be able to participate the way I usually do next year due to personal circumstances." Giving others as much time as possible to make alternative plans is both respectful and practical. If someone complains after the fact that they can't find someone to replace you, you can gently remind them that they have had months to work on the situation.

2. Keep a paper trail. Let me share with you an experience I had.

WHEN I WORKED FOR A SMALL TITLE 1 SCHOOL I HAD BEEN responsible for setting up and running all of the student study team (SST) meetings for four consecutive years. I had no special training and all of the meetings were held after school.

AFTER FOUR YEARS, I FOUND MYSELF OVERWHELMED AND NOT bringing my best energy to the meetings. At the beginning of year four, I made it very clear that this would be my last year accepting the duty. Every month I checked in with my administrator to remind them that I was happy to train my replacement. Predictably, as May rolled around, no replacement had been found. I had to put in writing, again, and copy the district office, that I would not be accepting this duty the following year and I was concerned that no action had been taken to find a replacement. OK, maybe that wasn't so gently reminding them. But it had effectively turned into a weird game of "chicken." It felt that the administrator was just hoping I'd change my mind, or thinking, "She'll never let the students go without SSTs."

You know what? I was a classroom teacher. Technically, my only responsibility was to complete SST referrals for my own students. The school not having a person to coordinate the meetings was an administrator's responsibility, not mine. Once the administrator realized they'd be running all of the meetings and that I was going to hold firm on my boundaries, a new teacher was found to take on the role.

Guess what? My replacement negotiated a stipend, and to have all SST meetings happen during the school day with substitute coverage for her class. I clearly should have taken a leaf from her book and set some boundaries on what my time was worth. I could be resentful about that, but not advocating for my needs and my worth sooner was a failing on my part. IT was a lesson I learned the hard way more than once.

Do I think that the administrator purposely took advantage of me? No. I think I was just a convenient answer to their problem and had the reputation of being highly competent, easygoing, and flexible. In this case, "highly flexible" and "easygoing" were synonymous with being a pushover. And that's on me.

3. Consider setting a boundary with limitations. Remember that participating doesn't need to be an "all or nothing" proposition. You can participate in a limited way, such as planning and coordinating but not being present at the event. If a stipend is involved you can consider splitting it.

In this section, we have examined how to avoid burnout and overwhelm by setting boundaries on how much time we work. We looked at ideas for how to reduce our workload through a combination of prioritization and productivity hacks and also gained confidence in professionally and comfortably setting boundaries with the amount of adjunct duties we commit to. In the next section, we will explore how to protect our energy and our peace by setting healthy boundaries with colleagues.

Beat Teacher Burnout with Better Boundaries

Yes/No Framework

By saying YES to this:

1.
2.
3.
4.

I'm saying NO to this:

1.
2.
3.
4.

By saying NO to this:

1.
2.
3.
4.

I'm saying YES to this:

1.
2.
3.
4.

Grace Stevens 2023

GRACE STEVENS

Declining "Professionally"

Grace Stevens 2023

Extra Duties Inventory

Make a list of all of the "extra" duties that you are currently involved in that go above and beyond your contractual obligations. For each one answer the questions. This should give you a "snap shot" of your current commitments.

Type of Commitment	Stipend Y/N Amount	Scale 1-10 of your PASSION for this	Committed through the end of the year? Y/N

Take a realistic look at this snapshot. Be honest about whether the committees and activities add joy and satisfaction to your life or leave you feeling depleted and resentful.

Grace Stevens 2023

5

Setting Boundaries with Co-Workers

There are several scenarios where you might need to set boundaries with your co-workers. Some of these situations involve co-workers who are your friends, maybe even your teaching besties. Other situations may involve co-workers who, let's face it, bother you. Just like we tell the students - you will not like everyone you have to work with, but you need to find a way to work productively and politely with them. Unlike our students, we're adults. We should be comfortable setting boundaries and being proactive about protecting our peace.

HERE ARE THE MAIN CATEGORIES OF CO-WORKERS WITH WHOM WE need to set boundaries:

- The Unscheduled Interrupter/Time Sucker
- The Toxic Complainer
- The Bossy Boots
- The Inappropriate Joker
- The Gossip

LET'S GO THROUGH THIS LIST ONE AT A TIME AND PRACTICE SOME sample scripts that can help you navigate setting boundaries.

AGAIN, IT'S HELPFUL TO PRACTICE THE SCRIPTS AND FIND THE words and phrasing that feel natural to you. Start with low-stakes situations so that you gain confidence before tackling more serious issues.

A QUICK NOTE ON A COLLEAGUE HAVING A "BAD DAY."

TEACHING IS HARD. SOME DAYS WE ARE PUSHED TO OUR LIMITS. None of us are superhuman and there are plenty of times that teachers, administrators, aides, parents, and students are just simply not our best selves.

WHILE I AM COACHING YOU ON HOW TO SET BOUNDARIES, IT'S NOT always appropriate to go all-out "boundary boss" on someone who is acting out of character and having a really tough time. Sometimes the only "boundary script" we need is a gentle word or two.

I AM A BIG BELIEVER IN EXTENDING PEOPLE GRACE AND ASSUMING that they have the best intentions. If someone who you usually get along fine with is uncharacteristically rude to you I would encourage you to take a kind, gentle approach before jumping to tell them that how they have spoken to you is unacceptable. Here's a simple phrase that can typically let a person know that they have crossed a line but without making them feel worse or defensive:

"Hey, are you OK? You don't usually snap at people like that."

"Hey, are you OK? It's unlike you to be so negative about a colleague."

Hey, are you OK? It's unlike you to say something mean-spirited like that."

In most instances, this more compassionate response will be enough for a colleague to check themselves and, most likely, apologize.

I know that for many of us if a colleague is rude to us our first instinct might be to just ignore it because we don't want to get involved in conflict. But this will lead to resentment and wanting to avoid the person. It is especially unhelpful if we later go off and complain to someone else, rather than directly address the issue with the person who has upset us. This just expands the bad energy and is not a very emotionally mature response. Sometimes a gentle,

"Hey, it's not cool to treat me like that, are you OK?"

is enough to spark a quick interaction and resolve the matter.

. . .

OK, IF THE "GENTLE TOUCH" HASN'T WORKED, OR THE PERSON IS A repeat offender, here are some specific scripts.

THE UNSCHEDULED INTERRUPTER/TIME SUCKER

Time suckers come in many forms. Left to their own devices, parents of students can fall into this category. There are so many boundaries that need to be set with parents to stop them from trampling all over you and your good nature that they have their own section in this book. So right now, let's focus on co-workers.

HERE IS THE FIRST SCENARIO. LET'S PRETEND THAT THE STARS ARE aligned, you are not covering anyone else's class or duty, and you finally have a prep period. You already have more than three hours' worth of tasks to squeeze into that precious 40-minute period, so there's no time to waste. Your bladder is empty, your computer is fired up, your flair pens are ready to go, and... a colleague walks in the door. They might have sought you out specifically, or your room may simply be part of the traffic pattern to get to the copy room, the coffee, the supply room, or the office. Either way, you are dealing with an unscheduled interruption, even if it is your teacher bestie.

THE CONVERSATION MAY START INNOCENTLY ENOUGH—AN anecdote about some crazy student behavior or unreasonable parent request. Before you know it, you are upping the ante with a war story of your own. Throw in some comments about how tired you are and how those ridiculous data reports are due, and you are off to the races. Before you know it, your prep period is over, and you have accomplished nothing. You end up frustrated at the situation and yourself.

HERE'S A SAMPLE BOUNDARY STRATEGY:

1. TELL THE PERSON YOU LOVE CHATTING WITH THEM.

2. Use "I" language to explain you have little self-control and lots of deadlines (remember, don't make people defensive by making this about their behavior - it's normal to stop and chat, after all!).

3. Suggest a time limit or an alternate arrangement.

HERE'S WHAT IT COULD SOUND LIKE:

"Hey, Susie, you know I love chatting with you. I have so much to do today, and I promised myself I would focus during my prep period. Let's set a timer for 5 minutes to catch up. Or how about we catch up at lunch on Wednesday?"

WHAT ABOUT THE PERSON WHO ALWAYS HAS QUESTIONS OR demands your time?

THIS IS A SCENARIO YOU CAN RELATE TO. THE INCREASING EXODUS of teachers from the field means that those teachers left have the burden of training, supporting, and "mentoring" all the new teachers who are coming in. Teachers with as little as one year of experience are suddenly in the position of being grade span or departmental leaders. I don't want to say it's the blind leading the blind, but it's the reality in many cases. Districts are so desperate for teachers they may have reduced the qualifications and training that were previously required for new teachers. This makes things extra stressful for new untrained, inexperienced teachers coming in and those left to pick up the slack. School can feel like a revolving door of new teachers who are thrown to the wolves, become overwhelmed, and quit. It's a sad and frustrating situation.

THIS LEAVES VETERAN TEACHERS WITH A DILEMMA. WE WANT TO give all the support we can, but we also need to protect ourselves from burnout and exhaustion.

HERE'S AN EXAMPLE. LAST YEAR I WAS PART OF A 4TH-GRADE TEAM of three. One teacher was brand new and completing her credential at night while she taught during the day. Not only could she not take on any extra duties because she was at school at night, but she was constantly overwhelmed while at school. The other teacher had some serious health concerns. Even though the other teacher and I did all of the lesson planning and put all of the lessons, slide decks, links, and teaching videos on a spreadsheet broken down by day and period, I would still receive, on average, 5-10 daily emails or texts from the new teacher. "How do I ____?" "Where is ____?" "How should I respond to this parent?" "What should I do with this student?"

IT WAS EXHAUSTING AND A CONSTANT INTERRUPTION TO MY teaching. Even worse, I was guilt-ridden that I couldn't give her more time and support, even though I felt I was holding her hand every step. I should have set a boundary sooner. I needed to stop being a victim and take control of the situation. I was getting resentful and annoyed, which was unfair to both of us and was not helping the situation. It was a lose-lose.

THE ADMINISTRATOR DID STEP UP AND GET THE NEW TEACHER MORE support from our curriculum coaches. Even though I was not officially her "mentor," but she still relied on me. It was her first instinct to email or text me before ever trying to find another resource or another way to find an answer. She asked the same questions repeatedly and was reluctant to adopt the organizational practices I suggested. If we met after school, the meetings were unstructured, she was unprepared, and they just dragged on.

EVENTUALLY, IT WAS AS SIMPLE AS THIS. I SUGGESTED THE TEAM SET up a weekly lunchtime meeting. At that time, we delegated tasks for the rest of the week. We set up meeting norms, including that no more than 5 minutes could be spent on "catching up."

We only had 40 minutes for lunch, and we knew when the bell went, the meeting would have to end. Any other time during the week that she texted or emailed me, I would simply ask, "Is this something you need right now, or can we discuss it on Wednesday?" If something couldn't wait, I would set a specific time and timeframe to address the issue. For example, "I can dedicate 5 minutes of my prep period to show you."

PROBLEM SOLVED. HERE ARE TAKEAWAY STRATEGIES:

1. Have a regularly scheduled meeting time to discuss issues and questions with colleagues.

2. Schedule the meeting when you know it will have a finite ending (i.e., during lunch or your prep period if you have one in common).

3. Set up meeting "norms" or agreements. This will be important when we discuss setting boundaries with Bossy Boots colleagues.

THE TOXIC COMPLAINERS AND BATTERY DRAINERS

If you are familiar with any of my work, you will know that a constant theme is that our energy teaches more than our lesson plans. A key component to student success in our classroom is that they enjoy being there, feel safe and valued, and that the teacher is also excited about being there and is committed to their success. That's a tall order for teachers. Bringing the best of yourself to your students every day is hard when you are overwhelmed, over-committed, resentful, irritable, and exhausted. Students sense our vibe, and they behave and engage accordingly.

THE POSITIVITY, ENTHUSIASM, AND PASSION WE BRING TO STUDENTS will affect their success more than the curriculum you have, your room decor, or whether your school has a Character Counts program. Setting boundaries to protect your peace and your energy is essential. Not only so you can have a more positive teaching experience, but so your students can have a more positive learning experience.

MANY THINGS EXHAUST AND DEMORALIZE US AS EDUCATORS, MOST of which we have no control over. But there is one area we have control over that is critical to maintaining our passion: limiting our exposure to toxic complainers and energy vampires. Every campus has them. They are the people who drain our emotional battery if we engage with them for too long.

Now, I'm not criticizing negative people. There are many things in education and the world to be negative about. Not all of us are naturally optimistic, resilient, and "glass half full" people. I'm not saying that being negative is wrong. I'm merely suggesting that it's not productive. And for those who work hard at maintaining an upbeat, proactive, and solution-oriented tempo, we need to set boundaries to protect our energy and outlook. We want to drain our batteries by doing fun things. We want to be exhausted because we played kickball with our class, ran with our dog, or crushed a Peleton class, not because we got cornered by the campus complainer.

I won't go into much detail about what constitutes a toxic complainer. You know who they are. We all vent once in a while. We are human, and we all need a safe space or teaching bestie to commiserate with. But there's a difference between someone having a bad day and someone who never has a positive word to say about any student, parent, co-worker, or situation. They complain for the sake of it and are not interested in any solutions you might offer.

Here's a bonus tip for you. Don't offer complainers unsolicited solutions. First, if people want advice, they'll ask for it. Second, toxic complainers will shoot unsolicited suggestions down. Your energy will be better spent working on your exit strategy from the conversation.

KEEP THIS SIMPLE. YOU KNOW THE PEOPLE WHO FILL YOU UP AND energize and inspire versus those who make you feel like you just wilted or aged ten years during your interaction. Just ask yourself the simple question, "When I interact with this person, do I end up feeling better or worse?" It doesn't need to be any more complicated than that.

HERE'S HOW YOU SET BOUNDARIES WITH THE TOXIC COMPLAINERS:

1. Acknowledge their pain. Their feelings are valid, and their experience is real to them. It is a basic human need to want to feel seen and validated.

2. Use "I" language.

3. Don't compete.

4. Extricate yourself from the conversation as lovingly and as soon as possible.

HERE ARE SOME VALIDATING STATEMENTS.

"Gosh, that sounds so hard!"

"Goodness, it sounds like you are having a challenging day!"

"Gracious, that would be upsetting to anybody!"

WHAT DO I MEAN BY "DON'T COMPETE"? WELL, RESIST THE URGE TO share a story of your own. Let's say someone says, "My student did the worst thing today!" Resist the urge to jump in and say, "Well, my student did this!"

Jumping in with your own story may be well-intentioned. You could be encouraging the person and letting them know they are not alone in their experience. You may be trying to show a shared connection with them, to empathize. The risk is that you could be perceived as invalidating them, trying to one-up them, or making the conversation about you. On a purely practical level, you prolong a conversation you don't want to be engaged in. So resist the temptation to share an anecdote about your student, your parent, your workload, how little you slept, or how exhausted you are.

Here's a sample boundary script:

"Gosh, that sounds hard. Listen, I need to get to a meeting/yard duty/the office, but I hope your day gets better!"

"Goodness, it sounds like that student is challenging. That's so hard. I have to get going, but I hope tomorrow is better. Get some good rest tonight!"

Let's move on to the next boundary crusher type - the co-worker, teammate, curriculum coach, or even parent who is very comfortable telling you what to do. This could also be the co-worker who has all kinds of opinions about what you do in your room or with your students that are none of their concern. Or the person with whom you need to collaborate who has to have everything exactly the way they want it. We'll call them:

. . .

THE BOSSY BOOTS

First, recognize that controlling behavior is related to setting personal boundaries and can be closely linked to over-functioning and codependency (which we will look at later). So Bossy Boots could benefit from exploring their boundaries, but that's not your concern. Your concern is setting healthy limits with them and their tendency to steamroll you, your contributions, and your ideas.

HERE ARE SOME STRATEGIES:

1. Avoid reacting. Controlling people are often looking for a reaction or to engage in confrontation, so make an extra effort to remain calm. Power struggles are neither pleasant, professional, nor productive.

2. Use "I" language and state your needs.

3. Be concise.

4. Acknowledge your worth.

5. Be prepared to follow through on a consequence.

HERE IS A SAMPLE SCRIPT:

"I feel disrespected when I am interrupted and when my ideas are immediately dismissed. I have as much to offer as everyone else on this team. I need to feel heard and respected. If I continue to be interrupted, I will request for this meeting to be continued via email." or "If I continue to feel invalidated, I will request a member of HR or admin sit in our next meeting."

. . .

You can try a less structured approach if you have to work with the person closely every day and generally share a friendly vibe.

1. Make the person aware of how you feel.
2. Try and gain consensus on a new approach.

"I feel my ideas are as valid as yours. We tried your way last time; let's try something new. What do you think?"

"I feel offended and condescended to when you use such an authoritative tone. We're teammates, right? I know we spend all day working with students, but the "teacher voice" doesn't work for me."

Those are some ideas for individuals. But what about when it's not a person being toxic but a group of people or a conversation in general?

Friends, you know where we are heading with this - straight into what my college professor always referred to as "the den of inequity" - the staff room or teacher's lounge.

The Inappropriate Joker

You know that awkward moment when someone is telling an offensive joke, and you are uncomfortable and waiting for someone else to say something? Well, those other people are equally awkward, hoping you will be the person to address the situation. Whether or not the inappropriate joke was directed at you, it would be the kind and professional thing to set a boundary with the offender.

First, it would be kind to the person telling the joke as they may be unaware that what they are saying is offensive. Also, your co-workers will feel relief and probably respect for your professionalism that you took a stand.

Sure, you could nervously laugh and walk away. But it's better to set a boundary, so you don't have to face the same situation repeatedly. It boils down to the same idea that we teach students about bullying. It's not enough not to bully; you need to be an "upstander" and support people who are being bullied. So even though we are not the person telling the inappropriate joke or saying unkind things about groups who have been historically marginalized, we are allowing them to continue.

I usually give people grace and assume they have the best intentions. You could casually call someone out on the fact that the joke is in appropriate.

For example:

"I know you might not mean harm, but those comments/jokes could get you in hot water with HR."

But if that doesn't work, you will need to be more direct.

. . .

Here are some strategies:

1. Be concise and clear that you find the joke offensive.

2. As always, use "I" statements. If others are present and uncomfortable, you might be able to use "we."

3. Make an explicit request.

4. If the person shrugs you off or tries to make you feel like a prude, all bets are off. You may resort to embarrassing them.

Here's what it might sound like:

"I don't find that joke funny. It's offensive and inappropriate for a work environment. Please don't tell that kind of joke here."

"I think some of us are feeling uncomfortable with that joke/comment. It's unkind and inappropriate to single out groups of people who have been discriminated against in the past. Please don't make comments like that here."

"I know you might not mean harm, but those comments/jokes could get you in hot water with HR."

What do I mean when I say a last resort might be to embarrass someone?

Well, imagine a scenario where there is a group of people. Lots of people find offensive jokes funny. It's a little passive-aggressive, but you could say,

"I DON'T GET IT. CAN YOU EXPLAIN TO ME WHY THAT'S FUNNY?"

THIS IS ALSO A GOOD RESPONSE IF THE JOKER ACCUSES YOU OF being a prude, uptight, or similar.

THE GOSSIP

Let's be honest. We should all have that one teacher best friend whom we can safely confide in, vent to, and laugh with. There is no teaching scenario where everyone on your campus is fantastic and exactly the type of person you love spending time with. Someone on campus will irritate you, treat students in a way you don't agree with, or even go out of their way to bully you. It could be a co-worker, an administrator, or a parent. Gossiping and venting to your teacher bestie about that person is an acceptable and necessary way to share feelings, get advice, and stay sane. Talking about the person/situation in the following places is not advisable:

- THE STAFF ROOM
- The hallways
- In writing (you never know when you might hit "reply all" on that email by mistake)
- On social media (people know people who know people who know the person you are talking about)

- The nail or hair salon (see above for the same reason)

QUICK STORY: I WAS GETTING MY NAILS DONE AT A BUSY LOCAL salon. A teacher from another school talked to the nail technician, told her about her terrible day, and shared all kinds of information about a student. Even though she didn't share his name, it was very unprofessional. My nail technician asked me about my day, and I kept my answers very general, like, "I love teaching. Some days are tough, but the students make it worth it!" When I got up to leave, I noticed that the mother of one of my most challenging students had been sitting at the station right behind me. I felt sick to my stomach. Honestly, it could have easily been me "venting" about a student or the school. I would have been mortified.

IT'S A SMALL WORLD. MY DAD WAS IN THE MERCHANT MARINES IN World War II. He drilled into me a million times the saying, "Loose lips sink ships!" I always hold onto that. Everyone needs to vent once in a while. But we must be mindful of what we talk about in public places. So that's it. Don't gossip. Set that boundary with yourself.

BUT WHAT ABOUT WHEN OTHER CO-WORKERS TRY TO DRAG YOU into their gossip session?

HERE ARE SOME EASY SCRIPTS.

Start by expressing your discomfort and try to change the conversation:

"I FEEL UNCOMFORTABLE LISTENING TO GOSSIP ABOUT OUR CO-worker. Can we talk about something else?" or

"I PREFER TO FOCUS ON MY WORK AND NOT GET INVOLVED IN gossip. Can we please talk about something else?"

OFFER AN ALTERNATIVE:

"I'm happy to talk about work-related topics, but let's avoid discussing our co-workers in a negative way."

EMPHASIZE THE IMPORTANCE OF RESPECT:

It's important to respect our co-workers and their privacy. Gossiping about them just doesn't sit well with me."

IF THEY CONTINUE, ENFORCE A BOUNDARY:

"I understand that you may have a different perspective, but I need to set this boundary for myself. I don't want to continue this conversation about our co-worker."

IF THE PERSON ISN'T GOSSIPING PER SE BUT COMPLAINING ABOUT another co-worker, you can ask,

"That sounds hard. Have you tried talking to them directly?"

This question will likely put them in a position where they have to admit they have not tried to resolve the situation with the other person and (hopefully) recognize that what they are doing is complaining and gossiping. You can set the boundary whether they want to acknowledge this or not:

"I'm uncomfortable talking about someone who isn't here to defend themselves. I have a policy of not saying anything about a person behind their back that I wouldn't feel comfortable saying to their face."

Remember our boundary rules - use "I" language.

When possible, don't have this conversation within earshot of other people. Your goal is to set a boundary for your peace and integrity, not to embarrass or shame someone.

In this section, we examined setting boundaries with colleagues that we work with. In the next section, we will look at how to set some boundaries with the parents and caregivers of our students. This is a critical area in avoiding burnout and reducing stress.

6

Setting Boundaries with Parents

Let me start by saying I have had positive, rewarding relationships with parents and caregivers for my entire teaching career. In twenty years, I can count on one hand the number of genuinely hostile and uncomfortable situations I've had to experience. I suspect some of this is because I came to teaching later in life, already had my own children, and had the experience of managing and working with people of all backgrounds. I always had confidence in this area, and many times parents who have been tricky for other teachers did not stress me out in the same way. I have been very fortunate that I have seldom had to set boundaries with parents regarding treating me respectfully, and I am sad to say that has not been the case for many of my colleagues.

However, one area of struggle with parents has been setting appropriate boundaries on my time.

. . .

Quick aside: I use the term "parents" for the sake of convenience. Like most teachers, many of my students have been raised by grandparents, foster parents, and even older siblings. When addressing students, I most often use the term "the adult in your home" or, when I taught first grade, "your grown-up."

I began teaching at a simpler time. Back in the day, if a parent wanted to reach me, they needed to call the school during regular school hours and leave a message.

Next came the era of voicemail. If I was teaching, a parent could leave a message on my classroom phone, and I could retrieve my messages during lunch or at the end of the day.

Then came email. Parents could send messages any hour of the day but generally expect an answer during school hours.

Finally, came parent communication apps that many of us have on our phones, such as Class Dojo, Remind, ParentSquare, etc. Parents can message us any time, on a device that we have in our hands or our pockets all day. The line separating school from home got a little blurred.

Then came COVID and distance teaching. Any semblance of boundaries between school and home was no longer blurred but obliterated. We were teaching from our homes into our students' homes, and parents were very comfortable stepping into the Zoom camera and talking with us or sending messages at all hours when students needed help accessing technology or completing assignments. Parents, teachers, and students were all wading into unprecedented territory, in survival mode, just trying to make it all work. We all saw more than we needed of each other's kitchens, bedrooms, and makeshift offices in basements, laundry rooms, or anywhere else we could try and work uninterrupted.

During distance teaching, we established some habits and practices that were essential at the time, but that were not sustainable. Being available to parents day and night no longer serves us. The time has come to boundary up and reestablish that line. School at school. Home at home.

As always, let's start with mindset.

You Are a Licensed Professional

In all likelihood, you invested a lot of time and money in becoming a credentialed teacher, administrator, counselor, or educator. You are a licensed professional just like a lawyer, doctor, or dentist. You have regular work hours for which you are financially compensated, and your employment contract with your school district dictates what those hours are. Essentially, you are performing your duties for free if you provide services, advice, meetings, and emails to parents outside these contracted hours.

. . .

LET ME ASK YOU THIS. DO YOU EXPECT YOUR DOCTOR, DENTIST, OR lawyer to provide you with their services free of charge? Probably not. So why is it okay for parents to assume that we will provide our services for free? Would you show up at your lawyer's office without an appointment, 5 minutes before they start their day or as they are leaving the office at night, and expect them to drop what they have planned and meet with you? Of course not. Then why do you allow parents to hi-jack your few precious prep minutes before or after school when they want to meet with you because it's convenient for them?

THERE WILL BE A FEW SPECIFIC CIRCUMSTANCES WHEN unscheduled meetings will be necessary and appropriate. But for the most part, you need to set a precedent where parents have an appointment to meet with you. This is for their benefit, as well as yours. You want to be sure you have the time to speak with them. You want to be sure you have the right resources in front of you. And for teachers in the primary grades who get hijacked daily as students are picked up and dropped off in person, you want to ensure confidentiality. It's never appropriate to discuss grades, behavior, or bullying in a doorway or gate when other parents and students are present.

I KNOW THIS MIGHT SOUND HARSH. IN THE FOLLOWING PAGES, I will give you many strategies for setting yourself up for success in this area and scripts that don't come across as aggressive or unprofessional. But this is the mindset piece for you. This is me bombing you with a little tough love. I've been there; I know it's hard, and it probably goes against your instinct to say "no" or set boundaries with parents.

. . .

Please don't let yourself be manipulated, or worse yet, bullied. Have the confidence to respond to the parent who has the nerve to tell you, "I pay my tax dollars; you work for me." It's important to respond professionally and in a non-defensive manner, but it is essential to respond and not just let that statement hang in the air awkwardly. You will find sample scripts later in this chapter.

First, let's look at setting yourself up for success so, hopefully, that the scripts will not be as necessary.

Manage Expectations

Proactively managing parent expectations will be your most effective tool in setting boundaries. Invest time at the beginning of the year letting parents know how to best communicate with you and when to expect a response. I usually share all of this at Back to School Night. As many parents do not attend this event, I make a short video explaining and showing them how to download the class/parent communication app.

1. Check with your school district's requirements concerning communication and grading policies. Ensure that whatever you communicate to parents is in line with the published guidelines. There will always be that one parent who has read every tiny section of the handbook and will call you to task. For example, most districts require that emails be responded to within 24 hours on school days. Other policies may dictate what is required of parents. For example, requests for independent studies should require 72-hour notice and not a

parent email at noon saying they want to "pick up work" at the end of the day.

2. GET BUY-IN FROM PARENTS. ASSURE THEM THAT YOU ARE committed to your students' success and meeting their needs. To do so, you must set up appropriate time boundaries. Find a way to communicate positively and diplomatically that you have limitations on your time because you are so committed to their success, not because you are lazy, burned out, or unwilling to go the extra mile. Most teachers go the extra mile. It's going the extra marathon that we need to avoid.

3. PROVIDE INFORMATION ABOUT YOUR PREFERRED METHOD OF communication and when and how parents should expect a reply. This will typically be by email or through a parent communication app such as Class Dojo, Remind, etc.

4. SET UP AND COMMUNICATE WHEN YOU HAVE STANDARD OFFICE hours. I always found it easier to be open to parent communication and meetings one afternoon a week so that I could plan accordingly. Exceptions will occur. But telling parents ahead of time that you have office hours on Wednesday from 3:30 - 4:30 PM eliminates a lot of unscheduled interruptions. Often if people have to wait until Wednesday, the situation may well have resolved itself.

5. SET UP "QUIET HOURS" ON YOUR PARENT COMMUNICATION APP SO that you do not receive notifications when you are at home or after a reasonable time. Every app has this ability. If you are not

sure how to do this, hop over to YouTube. Some kind soul will have a video showing you how to set it up.

6. EXPLAIN YOUR RATIONALE FOR PARENTS NEEDING AN appointment. Educate parents that unless it is an urgent or safety matter, it is unlikely that you will be able to see them the same day. Most parents are very reasonable. They are unaware that once students are dismissed, we start a whole other part of our job that involves meetings, committees, tutoring, adjunct duties, team planning, lesson planning, grading, etc. Also, reiterate confidentiality and the importance of avoiding impromptu meetings in doorways and gates.

OF COURSE, SETTING UP EXPECTATIONS AND ENFORCING THEM ARE not the same thing. Be extra diligent at the beginning of the year. Like students, many parents are what I refer to as "boundary researchers." They will blow through your preferences or think they don't apply to them. Preferences only become boundaries when we consistently enforce them. An innocent "Can I talk to you for a minute?" request at the gate can quickly turn into a 45-minute meeting you weren't planning. It may also set a precedent for that parent and others observing the interaction that impromptu meetings are acceptable.

BE PROACTIVE WITH COMMUNICATION

Another way to set yourself up for success is to have a consistent process for proactively sharing information. I suggest a classroom/parent communication app for a few reasons.

. . .

1. Parents don't always read emails but usually have their phones with them and will open the app if they get notifications.

2. The app provides a "paper trail" of texts and messages and the ability to document if the parent viewed the message.

3. Ease of adding photos and video straight from your phone. It takes 5 minutes to record and send a video versus considerably longer to write an email.

4. Ability to have numerous contacts for each child so that if mom, dad, and grandma want access to information, you don't need to make multiple copies.

I have used Class Dojo for about five years. It's an excellent app for classroom management (randomizer, assigning reward points, and sharing portfolios are just a few features), but the real magic happens when I use it for parent communication. I'm sure all apps have similar features, and here are some ways I use them to reduce parent emails significantly.

On Monday, when I hand the students their homework check-off sheet for the week, I take a photo of it and send it to all the parents with one click. No more emails asking me about dues dates or details.

On Fridays, before I go home, I make a quick video about upcoming due dates, projects, or anything they need to know about the following week. We're not talking about high-production value videos. Open the app, hit record, and talk. No one is going to be concerned with lighting or sound quality. Of course, parents have access to my class website, the school website, and Google Classroom, where all of this information can also be found. But having it on an app seems more appealing to many parents.

Whenever a parent emails or sends a message asking about things I've already communicated, I tell them, "Please refer to the video I sent on Friday and let me know if you have additional questions." Copy, and paste. Done.

Before you tell me that your parents won't use an app, yes, they will, if you make it a requirement. On Back to School Night, I say, "In this class, we use this app. Let's set it up on your phone right now." It's like saying, "We use Google Classroom." It's what we do. Someone in their household likely has a smartphone if they don't. Reassure them that if they know how to send texts, they know how to use the app. On a side note, I worked in a school where many parents were not raised in the US and lacked confidence in reading and writing in English. They assured me that the weekly videos were very helpful.

Boundary Scripts for Pushy Parents

Being proactive and communicating expectations will eliminate many parent emails. Again, I'm not against parent emails, and I want my students to feel safe and successful and work with parents and help them support their child's learning. It's the time wasters and entitled parents who try to take advantage of our naturally giving nature or intimidate us that we are concerned about here.

HERE ARE SOME SAMPLE SCRIPTS.

NOTE: IF YOU ARE RESPONDING TO PARENT EMAILS, ALWAYS START with:

"Dear ….. I am committed to (name)'s success and appreciate you reaching out to me."

YOU NEVER WANT TO GIVE PARENTS THE IMPRESSION THAT THEY are bothering you. But you do need to set boundaries.

AS A GENERAL RULE, FOLLOW THESE STEPS:

1. Acknowledge the concern

2. Use "I" language

3. Explain your availability (Remember, don't apologize. You can use those magic words, "As it turns out...")

4. Provide alternatives

5. Reassure parents you are committed to their child's success and want to work together as a team to ensure it

HERE'S WHAT IT MIGHT SOUND LIKE:

THE PARENT WHO WANTS TO MEET WITH YOU IN THE DOORWAY.

"I understand that you would like to discuss this right now.

As it turns out, I have a full schedule today. I would be happy to schedule a time to meet with you to give this matter the time and attention it needs and to ensure student confidentiality.

I have office hours available on Wednesday afternoon. If we need to talk before then, I will check my schedule and email you some options tomorrow morning. Or you could address the matter by email.

If you feel the matter is urgent or a safety concern, I encourage you to talk to the office.

I am committed to your child's success, and I'm confident we can work this out."

The parent who is questioning a grade.

"Thank you for bringing this to my attention.

I understand that you are concerned about your child's grade. So am I!

While grades are important, focusing on your child's effort and progress is also important.

I have spent a lot of time providing constructive and detailed feedback to your child in class and have given them the time and opportunity to revise and improve their grade.

Once you have discussed this with your child, let me know if you would like to schedule a quick phone call. We can discuss how we can work together to ensure your child gets the support they need, taking responsibility for their effort, and how we can work together to ensure their success.

Here are three 15-minute time slots that I have available this week."

The parent who wants last-minute work or a last-minute independent study.

"Thanks for reaching out to me. That's great to learn you are going to Disneyland for a week. What a fun experience for you all!

Please refer to the school policy on requesting independent studies. As teachers have many responsibilities and packed schedules, the school has a policy that requires advance notice for additional work requests. I am unable to produce an independent study by tomorrow.

Please check with the office as to what they suggest your child does to complete the missing work on their return. In the meantime, here are some additional online resources your child can access.

I hope you have a great trip and make many precious memories."

Note, if you have all your assignments in Google Classroom or something similar, you can explain to the parent that the student will get credit for any assignments they complete independently.

The parent who wants information so they can confront another student or parent about bullying.

"Thank you for reaching out to me. As a teacher, it's my responsibility to create a safe and inclusive learning environment for all my students. I take all reports of bullying seriously and will address any concerns or incidents that come to my attention.

If your child has experienced or witnessed bullying, please encourage them to speak with another trusted adult or me so that we can take appropriate action.

I am happy to work with your child to resolve this issue and to get administrators involved if the situation warrants this. The school has protocols in place and will communicate with the necessary students and parents.

Per school policy, I am unable to disclose personal information about other students or parents, and it's important to protect the privacy and confidentiality of all individuals involved.

If you have additional concerns, I encourage you to contact the office."

The parent who wants to be your "friend" on social media.

"Thank you for reaching out to me. I understand that you would like to connect with me on social media.

As a teacher, I need to maintain professional boundaries with my students and their parents. While I'm happy to communicate with you through email or other school-approved channels, I prefer to keep my personal life private and do not accept social media friend requests from parents.

Please don't take this personally, as this is a universal boundary I have set for myself after seeing some negative things happen to co-workers.

Of course, if you have any concerns or questions about your child's education, please don't hesitate to reach out to me through email or phone. You can also schedule a meeting with me through the school's scheduling system.

I am fully committed to student success and will always support them and you in a professional capacity."

There will be other scenarios where you need to set boundaries with parents. Remember, it is important to validate people's concerns, hold firm on your boundaries, and communicate them in a matter-of-fact way.

The parent who is becoming hostile or says, "I'm a taxpayer; you work for me!"

"I notice that you seem very upset. I understand that you may have strong feelings about your child's education, but it's not appropriate for you to speak to me in a hostile or aggressive manner.

I too am a taxpayer. Technically speaking, I work for a school district. If there are specific policies that you disagree with, I encourage you to participate in parent club and school board meetings. We are always in need of passionate individuals.

. . .

If you would like to discuss concerns about your child with me, I encourage you to schedule an appointment. I would be happy to talk with you when you (or we) have calmed down and can talk respectfully and professionally.

I am stepping away from this conversation until we can discuss this in an appropriate manner."

Remember, things will go much smoother if you start the year by communicating expectations. But if you read this mid-year, you can still make positive changes.

Here are some other tips to consider to set yourself up for success.

1. Assume the best intentions. Parents are just as busy, overwhelmed, and stressed as we are. They may genuinely be unaware that what they are requesting is unreasonable. Calmly and politely state the policy or boundary.

2. Don't take things personally. You have 20-35 students in your class to worry about. (or up to 200 if you teach higher grades). The parent only has one in your class, and it's their baby. That child is likely the most important thing in their lives. Don't take it personally if they aggressively "Mama Bear" on you.

3. Understand that the parent may not have all the facts. Let's concede that students are not always reliable narrators of a

situation. The parent may have gotten a biased or embellished version of what happened.

4. DON'T RESPOND TO EMAILS OR MESSAGES WHEN UPSET OR triggered. Wait until you are calm and have a co-worker proofread what you have written. If a parent is upsetting you in person by being aggressive, use some version of the scripts above.

5. BE CONSISTENT! IF YOU HAVE A RULE OR BOUNDARY, YOU NEED to enforce it consistently. For example, you should not deny one parent a last-minute request for work but go out of your way to accommodate another parent because you have a better relationship with them or had one of their other children in the past. You will be perceived as playing favorites which is unprofessional and can lead to a significant amount of stress if parents start calling you out in person or on social media.

THE CASE FOR WITNESSES

Lastly, if you fear that a parent meeting may get heated or hostile, set a boundary that you will need either an administrator or, at the very least, a co-teacher or aide to be in the meeting. You can present this to the parent as wanting someone in the room to take notes so that you can give them your undivided attention. What you are doing with this is ensuring that you have a witness and procuring written documentation because you never know when you might need it.

. . .

BEFORE I MOVE ON TO SETTING BOUNDARIES WITH STUDENTS, I want to remind you that this information is designed to empower you. Again, I can count on less than one hand the times I've had truly difficult interactions with parents. Your boundary setting with parents will mostly involve limiting their access to you and your time, not hostile conversations.

REMEMBER, EVERYONE HAS THE SAME GOAL- PROVIDING THE BEST educational experience for their child. This can only be accomplished if you protect your time and energy so that you have time to plan appropriately and show up as your best self for your students every day. You need to set these boundaries so that you can support your students in positive ways, and no reasonable parent should argue with that.

7

Setting Boundaries with Students

This is not a book about classroom management. But all classroom management, one way or another, boils down to boundaries. Many students who "act out" are crying out for boundaries.

YES, THAT IS A BROAD STATEMENT; NOT EVERY STUDENT WITH behavior issues will fall into this category. But over my two decades in the classroom, the majority of which were at a Title 1 school, this was true in my experience. Students with chaotic home lives where boundaries were missing or inconsistent continually tested class boundaries for the first few weeks of school. Many came in with the attitude: "When the teacher says no, does she mean it? Let's test that." Some students were more aggressive researchers than others. But once they realized that the standards, expectations, and procedures were consistent, a sense of security set in, and they felt calmer, and many of the behaviors disappeared.

. . .

So that's the mindset piece. Classroom management is all about setting boundaries. You could call them rules; you could call them standards. But how you, as the teacher, set and enforce boundaries will be the biggest determining factor of how smoothly your day with students goes.

I'll say it again. *Your energy teaches more than your lesson plans.* A teacher who is calm and confident in their ability to manage disruptions and who is energized and organized (which only happens if you have set appropriate boundaries on your time) provides a very different teaching experience for their students. Students respond accordingly. They are more engaged and less likely to test the limits.

It is also helpful to recognize that the students who challenge us the most often stretch us to grow. Positively impacting the lives of struggling students is one of the most rewarding aspects of teaching and what gets us out of bed in the morning. There is no dream class where all the students are compliant, engaged, and academically proficient. Let go of that fantasy. Recognize that you can have a positive teaching experience with the students you have, the grade assignment you have, the physical classroom you have, and the co-workers you have if you get good at setting boundaries.

Getting Student Buy-In

Students will be more open to following rules and respecting boundaries if they feel they have a voice in creating them. For the last six or so years of teaching, I gave up actual "rules" in favor of standards.

I asked students to think about the learning environment they wanted to create. I would give them sticky notes and ask them to come up with one word. Typical words that came up were: fun, friendly, respectful, quiet, supportive, and safe. I would have a few sticky notes of my own in the event that some of my preferred words weren't identified. Terms such as collaborative, considerate, and responsible. After everyone had a word, I would ask them to write two things that helped them learn in class and two things that got in the way of their learning.

From this feedback, I presented our standards (I usually have the same ones), and each student could put one "word" next to the standards they thought best applied to it. In this way, they could see that the standards are there to support everyone's learning so everyone's needs can be met.

As the teacher, you will realize that the standards cover any undesirable behavior you want to eliminate. Four standards are much more student-friendly than having a long list of rules. We recited them and revisited them often. The standards I used were modified from a Project GLAD (Guided Language Acquisition Design) training I participated in many years ago. Feel free to use these or create your own. Here they are:

1. Show Respect

2. Make Good Decisions

3. Solve the Problem

4. Take Responsibility for Your Learning

Whether choosing standards or rules, make sure the language is clear, concise, and positive.

Once you set your standards and establish student buy-in, it's time to learn how to enforce them. What follows are three magical words to help you. They have served me well through two decades of teaching other people's children and almost three decades of raising my own.

I was first introduced to these words by a dear friend who is a child psychologist. We were in a car with my first child, a few months old, in her car seat. I don't have younger siblings or cousins, I wasn't a teacher yet, and had honestly never been around babies. I felt low-key freaked out and massively underqualified for this enormous new responsibility. So I asked him, "What's the best advice you can give me not to mess her up?" He just gave me three magic words:

Calm. Consistent. Consequences.

The 3 Magic C's of Classroom Management

Calm

Let's talk about staying calm. Goodness knows that some students are what I call my "spiritual practice." They will try and push every button they can, and you need the patience of a saint to stay calm and professional. But doing so is essential. First, because your blood pressure and health depend on it. Second, because students respond to your energy. If your voice becomes louder and your body language and expressions show rising anger or frustration, the situation will only escalate.

HERE ARE SOME TIPS TO HELP YOU REMAIN CALM:

1. Set boundaries in all areas of your life.

Overwhelm and frustration will have less chance to take over if you are well-rested and happy to be at school. Proper self-care is showing up as your best self so that you can handle challenging situations with grace and professionalism.

2. DON'T ENGAGE.

Say what you have to say calmly, respectfully, and clearly. Don't start arguing with a student. Remember, you are the adult. It's a normal part of development for students to lack self-regulation, but you are a professional. You should be calm and remain entirely in control of the situation. Engaging in a power struggle is inappropriate and ineffective. You risk backing students into a corner where they don't want to lose face in front of their peers and continue to escalate the situation.

3. DON'T TAKE STUDENT BEHAVIORS OR COMMENTS PERSONALLY.

Students may test boundaries if they are experiencing stress or other personal challenges and may act out as a way of coping with their emotions. If their life is chaotic, your classroom may be the only place they feel safe to vent their frustrations. In many cases, students who feel powerless in other areas of their lives will try to exert control or get attention in maladaptive ways. It always helps me to view classroom disruptions and behaviors as a cry for help. I reframe students being "needy" and wanting attention to students craving connection. In many cases, poor classroom behavior isn't a result of malice; it's a result of trauma.

IF THE BEHAVIORS ARE EXTREME OR REPEATED, YOU WILL NEED TO take appropriate action. That might include student study teams and referrals if you feel a student could benefit from counseling or social skills intervention. Be proactive about getting students the support they need. Don't just pray you can make it through 180 days of interacting with a student. Move beyond how they perform and act in your class and be concerned about how they will perform and act in life. You could be the teacher that changes everything for a student.

REMEMBER THAT STUDENTS TESTING THE WATERS IS A NORMAL PART of human development as they learn to assert their independence. Again, it's not you, it's biology, and it comes with the teaching territory.

YOU MAY NOTICE THAT NONE OF THESE TIPS ON REMAINING CALM are "count to ten silently when you feel yourself getting worked up." Not that there is anything wrong with counting to ten. But the goal is to avoid getting worked up in the first place.

CALM IS BEING IN CONTROL OF EMOTIONAL REACTIVITY, AND IT stems from self-assurance, practice, and self-care in all areas of your life. But if you feel emotions rising, there is nothing wrong with stepping away for your own time-out and telling the student, "We will discuss this after class." And make a conscious choice to lower your voice when doing so.

Now let's talk about being consistent.

Consistent

Let's define what consistency in a classroom looks like. It means that if you have a rule or standard, you enforce it calmly, confidently, and respectfully every single time. Regardless of who the student is. Regardless of what mood you are in. If the rule is one verbal warning, then a consequence, you need to be prepared to follow through every single time. If you don't, those aggressive researchers will keep testing the boundaries, and it will become a game or challenge for them.

Consistency is also vital for other reasons.

First, it's a fairness issue. If students perceive that you have different rules for different students, they will start thinking of themselves as being in either one of two camps - the teacher's favorite students or the students who are picked on. This can be very damaging to a sense of classroom community and can also expose you to criticism and complaints. You don't want to have to defend yourself to a parent whose child goes home and says they feel singled out and punished for things that other students get away with.

. . .

NEXT, BEING INCONSISTENT IS THE LEAST EFFECTIVE AND MOST stressful classroom management style.

HERE'S SOMETHING I REMEMBER VERY CLEARLY FROM MY CHILD development classes. It was data that of the three main parenting styles- authoritarian, permissive, and inconsistent, the latter is the most damaging. When children are unaware of limits and when consequences are randomly enforced, they can become anxious and have attachment issues. Chaotic and unpredictable parenting, alternating between affection and bribes and then yelling and harsh punishment, can leave children uncertain about the world's rules and how to follow them correctly.

THINK OF HOW THIS PLAYS OUT IN A CLASSROOM.

SOME TEACHERS SURVIVE BY BEING COMPLETELY AUTHORITARIAN. They are uncompromising, inflexible, and have a reputation for instilling fear. The "I would rather be feared than loved" teachers. Other teachers have reputations for being overly lenient. They may present as wanting to be friends with their students. As a result, their classrooms may be loud and chaotic and cause stress for quiet, compliant students who want to get their work done.

HOWEVER, THE TEACHERS WHO STRUGGLE THE MOST ARE THE ONES who are inconsistent. They are overwhelmed, exhausted, stressed, and constantly repeat themselves. They try to negotiate or bribe students to behave. They nag, raise their voice, plead, and even try to shame students into behaving. When their frustration finally gets the best of them, they hand out random consequences that they don't really want to enforce, and students know this. Have you ever told students they lost recess and then, realizing you needed to cover the yard or didn't want to lose your break to stay in the room with your class, give them a way to earn recess back? We've all been there. It's like a parent yelling, "I'm canceling Christmas!" Everyone knows you are unlikely to follow through on your threat.

Such inconsistencies are counterproductive and perpetuate a vicious cycle of misery as students start viewing boundaries as flexible and continue to challenge them.

Consequences

Boundaries come with consequences for violating them. This is never more true than when working with students. I like to tell students that choices are like actions in science. We learn that every action has a reaction. Likewise, every choice has a consequence. The consequence could be positive or negative. Consequences is a rather dramatic word. I like to consider it nothing more than giving students feedback on how they are doing.

Educators have different opinions about consequences. Some teachers go all in with a classroom token economy or school-wide PBIS (Positive Behavior Interventions and Supports) program where students earn rewards for positive behavior. Others argue that intrinsic motivation is more effective than extrinsic motivation and that rewarding students for things they should be doing anyway constitutes manipulation. So, depending on where you stand, you may limit positive consequences to telling students that they've done a good job or should be proud of themselves. However, no teacher or campus can avoid enforcing consequences for negative behaviors.

RESTORATIVE JUSTICE

In recent years, there has been an increase in the practice of restorative justice in education. Restorative justice is a philosophy and approach to justice that focuses on repairing the harm caused by crime or conflict rather than simply punishing the offender. It can be used as an alternative to traditional discipline approaches, such as suspension or expulsion.

THERE ARE SEVERAL REASONS WHY RESTORATIVE JUSTICE IS A GOOD idea in education.

FIRST, IT HELPS TO BUILD RELATIONSHIPS AND PROMOTE A SENSE OF community within the school. When students are involved in conflicts or misbehavior, restorative justice approaches allow them to take responsibility for their actions and make amends with those they have harmed rather than simply being punished and isolated. This can help students to develop empathy and understand the impact of their actions on others.

SECOND, RESTORATIVE JUSTICE CAN MORE EFFECTIVELY ADDRESS the root causes of misbehavior. Traditional discipline approaches often fail to address the underlying issues contributing to misconduct, such as trauma, stress, or family problems. On the other hand, restorative justice approaches involve students in finding solutions and addressing the underlying issues, which can be more effective at preventing future misbehavior.

Finally, restorative justice can help to reduce the school-to-prison pipeline.

A reduced number of students being suspended or expelled results in fewer students entering the criminal justice system. Restorative justice programs provide alternative approaches to discipline that focus on repair and reconciliation rather than punishment and exclusion.

Logical Consequences

Whether or not you have a restorative justice program at your school, everyone can agree that consequences should be logical. Logical consequences are directly related to misbehavior and are intended to teach students the natural consequences of their actions. The idea behind consequences should be to teach and reinforce acceptable behavior, not to punish students. Using logical consequences, teachers can help students understand the natural consequences of their actions and encourage them to take responsibility for their behavior.

Students should be aware of the consequences so there are no surprises. Again, you should avoid generic consequences such as "Go to the office!" or "You have detention!" unless that is the automatic consequence assigned to the severity of the offense—

no need to cancel recess for the whole class because two students were too chatty.

HERE ARE SOME EXAMPLES OF LOGICAL CONSEQUENCES.

LET'S SAY A YOUNGER STUDENT ISN'T FOLLOWING PLAYGROUND rules or play equipment rules. The logical consequence would be that they cannot play with the equipment or on the yard for a certain amount of time.

IN THIS INSTANCE, SETTING THE BOUNDARY WOULD BE AS SIMPLE AS communicating the rule (yes, give them the benefit of the doubt that they forgot) and telling the student what the consequence would be if they choose to break it.

"THE RULE IS FEET FIRST ON THE SLIDE, ONE STUDENT AT A TIME. IF you break the rule again, you will not be able to play on the equipment for the rest of recess."

That's it. Then follow through consistently. No need to nag or criticize. No need to add, "Why don't you listen? I'm tired of telling you this every day!"

1. STATE THE RULE.
2. State the consequence.

3. Be prepared to enforce the consequence. Every time. With every student.

Here are some more examples. If students cause a mess in the cafeteria, they should miss their lunch recess and have to clean it up. If they chew gum, they need to spend time cleaning up gummy messes from under desks and on the playground.

Let's look at an example for older students. What if a student cusses in class?

"The rule is that we speak to each other respectfully and with appropriate language. Using bad language is not only disrespectful to others, but it can also create a negative and unproductive learning environment. If you use bad language again, you will be required to complete a reflective writing assignment about the impact of your words on others."

Let's say a student is having trouble staying on task or is constantly talking. You can have them sit at a quiet table for a while, a desk in isolation and beyond earshot of their friend zone.

Some of you may be eye-rolling and thinking, "This is pretty obvious stuff." Yes, this is standard practice. But I invite you to honestly reflect on how you set boundaries with your students.

. . .

Are you calm and consistent *every time?*

Do you *always* give concise instructions or reminders of what the rule is?

Are you guilty of making non-specific requests such as:

"You guys, settle down!"

As I once had to point out to a student teacher I was training, yelling "Shh!" repeatedly is not an effective classroom management technique.

Are you guilty of asking rhetorical questions or criticizing? For example:

"Why do you guys never listen?"

"How many times do I need to repeat myself?"

Is it evident to your students when your frustration level is rising?

We are all human, and none of us have an infinite sense of patience. But sometimes we must reflect and ask ourselves: "Is the reason my class is out of control 100% about what the students are doing or is some of this a result of what I am or am not doing?" Take ownership.

. . .

Remember, the perfect dream class doesn't exist. But you should be in control of the classroom. You are 100% capable of communicating and enforcing effective boundaries, and investing time in practicing how to do so will benefit not only you but also your students.

Boundary Scripts for Students

Here are some sample scripts for common situations you may run into where additional boundaries beyond your classroom rules and standards may be required.

Because there is a different power dynamic in play in these interactions, the scripts are more direct. The adults set the rules, and the students comply.

We don't communicate the dynamic in those words, but it is implied. More often, our tone and confidence communicate more than our actual words.

When we set boundaries with students, we are usually giving instructions or explaining the consequences. Therefore the language is often no longer "I" (about my behavior) but "you" (about things you, the student, need to do). However, remember that the conversation should always be about the behavior, not the child. The goal should always be to communicate a boundary and a consequence; it should never be about berating, nagging, or shaming a child.

SOME TEACHERS START WITH "I NEED YOU TO" BEFORE GIVING instructions. So you can try those words and see if they feel authentic. Everyone has their preferred style of communicating with students but remember the three Cs: Calm. Consistent. Consequences.

HERE ARE SOME SAMPLE SCRIPTS FOR EVERYDAY SITUATIONS YOU may run into where additional boundaries beyond your classroom rules and standards may be required.

SCENARIO: A STUDENT IS TALKING BACK TO YOU IN CLASS.

1 ACKNOWLEDGE THE STUDENT'S FEELINGS: "I UNDERSTAND THAT you may feel frustrated or upset, but it's not OK to speak to me that way."

2 Set a boundary: "I expect you to show respect and speak to other adults and me in a polite and appropriate manner."

3 Consequences: "If you continue to talk back to me, there will be consequences. This could include a loss of privileges, a referral to the principal, or other disciplinary action."

4 Offer support: "I'm here to help you succeed and be successful in school. Please let me know if you're having trouble with the material or have any other concerns. I'm happy to work with you to find solutions."

5 Follow through on the consequence if necessary: "I understand that you may disagree with this consequence, but it's important that you meet the expectations of the class and show respect to authority figures. If you continue to talk back, I will have to follow through on the disciplinary action we discussed."

So, that's a lot to have to say all the time. After the first time, it can go like this:

"I sense you are getting frustrated. It's okay to be frustrated, but it's not okay to talk to me disrespectfully. We will both step away from this conversation for a few minutes. At that time, if you are still disrespectful to me, (state your consequence)."

Another quick way to handle a student who wants to "engage" is to offer to continue the discussion on their time, not on class time. Now, this will also be during your free time, so, understandably, you may be reluctant to go down this path. But here's the script:

"I sense you are overwhelmed/frustrated/ not in agreement with me (whatever the situation is). It's okay to be overwhelmed but it's not to talk to me in a disrespectful tone. I am stepping away, and we will continue this conversation during recess/lunch/after school."

. . .

Scenario: A student asks to connect with you on social media.

"That's nice of you to ask. However, as your teacher, I need to maintain professional boundaries with students. I'm happy to communicate with you through email or other school-approved channels for academic purposes."

"Please don't take it personally. I value my privacy and have a policy of not accepting social media friend requests from students or parents."

Be sure to check your school policy. Many districts have a policy regarding this. It can be an easy out for you to say, "The district policy prohibits it. Sorry!"

Scenario: A student asking you overly personal questions.

Note: I've heard it all from the innocent "How many children do you have?" (OK to answer) to the inappropriate "Why don't you have a wedding ring?" (under no obligation to answer), all the way through to the questions you know have been discussed at the dinner table and smack of parental snooping, such as "Do you have tattoos?" "Do you go to church?" and even, "Are you even an American citizen?"

Here's what you can say:

"I understand that you may be curious about my personal life, but respecting my boundaries is important. I only share what I feel is appropriate about my private life. I'm here to support you and your learning, and I'm happy to answer any questions you have about the course material or other academic topics."

PART III

Setting Boundaries with Family and Friends

8

Protecting Your Peace Outside of School

Once you become more comfortable with setting boundaries around your teaching career and realize how much they positively impact your physical, mental, and emotional health, you may wish to set setting more healthy boundaries in other areas of your life.

As noted before, setting boundaries can improve *all* your relationships, including with your family and friends. But this does need to be handled with a more delicate hand.

You may feel resistant to setting better boundaries in your personal relationships, fearing it might jeopardize them. Maybe you anticipate pushback from people who have become used to your habit patterns. This is a legitimate concern. The people closest to you might feel that the delegation of duties or your reluctance to advocate for your own needs has been fine and may be unwilling to adopt new rules of engagement that don't benefit them as much. Depending on how gently you proceed and present your new boundaries, some people in your life may also see it as a betrayal of some unspoken pact between you.

Mindset

Approach any conversations with the right intention. Remind yourself and others that the goal in setting boundaries is to enrich your relationship and establish healthy patterns. You are taking the time to set boundaries because you value the relationship, and you want both you and the other person to feel appreciated and respected.

Remember to start with situations, preferences, and requests that are lower stakes or have less emotional charge around them. Starting with the issue that you are struggling most with in a relationship is going to lead to a lot of anxiety, and you may find it hard to remain calm and gentle in your approach.

Setting boundaries with people you love should not be about nagging or controlling. The easiest place to start could be with situations where you don't say "no" outright, but you say "yes" with limits.

Remind yourself about everyone's boundary rights:

- You have a right to say no without guilt.
- You have a right to be treated respectfully.
- You have a right to put your needs on par with someone else's.

- You have a right to accept your mistakes and flaws.

- You have a right to reject other people's unreasonable expectations.

- You have the right to change your mind.

Here are some other mindsets and tips to remember before embarking on conversations.

Boundaries are about your needs and preferences, not just your non-negotiables (deal breakers).

Remember to focus on "I" statements. For example, "I feel overwhelmed when…" instead of "When you do this…"

People tend to get more defensive when you use absolutes such as "always" or "never." It's unlikely that someone always does something, and using absolutes can lead to people feeling attacked. It's important to avoid the conversation deteriorating into a list of your partner's shortcomings.

Be aware of your tone. How you approach a conversation with your children about boundaries will be very different from how you approach your partner, your siblings, or your parents.

Below are some sample boundary scripts. However, if you are setting boundaries with relationships that are important to you, I would also advise learning about Marshall Rosenberg's "Non-Violent Communication" (NVC) framework.

Non-Violent Communication Framework

Please don't be put off by the name. It's not a framework for situations where you are afraid that setting boundaries or having hard conversations will end in a physical fight. NVC is concerned with communicating with empathy and understanding, to transform relationships for the better. Instead of approaching tough conversations with language and a mindset that is divisive (win/lose), it's about seeking collaboration in finding a solution.

There are 4 basic elements to NVC. You will find a helpful PDF graphic in the Workbook. The steps are:

1. Observation. Bring attention to the issue without criticism or judgment by simply stating, "I notice" or "When I hear you say"

2. State how it makes you feel, "I feel"

3. State your need, "Because I need"

4. Make the request, "Would you please?" and/or enlist their input on a solution, "How do you think we can resolve this?" "What do you think we could do so that both our needs are met?" (Hint: an excellent place to start might be a boundary with limitations)

For example,

. . .

"I notice when we are eating together you often have your phone in your hand, or on the table checking messages."

"This makes me feel that you are distracted and I'm eating alone. I look forward to spending time with you and our conversations at the dinner table, and I need to feel that you are present with me."

"How about we agree to leave our phones on the counter when we eat and not look at them or answer any calls until we've both finished eating and clearing up together?" or

"I'm requesting that we leave our phones on the counter when we are eating together."

I did not invent this framework. You can find many examples of Dr. Rosenberg's work online. For a deeper dive, you can check out the book:

Nonviolent Communication: A Language of Life: Life-Changing Tools for Healthy Relationships, Marshall Rosenberg PhD

Or visit the Center for Non-Violent Communication at https://www.cnvc.org/

. . .

Boundary Scripts

As the focus of this book is to look at boundaries through the lens of a teacher or an educator, here are some likely boundary scenarios that may come up in your personal life uniquely about teaching.

First, unless you have other family members who are educators, you may receive pushback about the number of hours you work. It's one of the areas that causes a lot of stress for families and partners of educators.

Remember that this concern (complaint) is probably very valid. In all likelihood, even if you are getting better at setting boundaries at work, you will frequently have more work to do than can be completed within contract hours and extra duties you need to take on. Being consistently reminded of how many extra hours you work and how that affects others doesn't help.

Here's what you can say.

"I understand that I work many hours outside of my contract, and that impacts our family time and extra household duties that you need to take on."

"I feel extra stressed and guilty when you bring this up."

. . .

"Please know that teaching is very important to me, and I accept that it comes with extra responsibilities and commitments. I value our time together and am setting boundaries at work to make it a priority. Thanks for being patient. It means the world to me."

Another situation that may sound familiar is that of extended family demands during school breaks. Teachers typically crawl their way into any significant break or school holiday and arrive at the finish line exhausted. We often want to just relax, catch up on some sleep or organizing, and not rush off to some large family gathering, especially if it is out of town and involves travel. This is especially true if you feel bullied or marginalized by members of your extended family who don't understand how challenging and all-consuming teaching can be.

Maybe you are trying hard to break through unhealthy family patterns and create new family traditions and memories with your immediate family unit. Maybe you don't want to deal with marshmallow salad and terrible holiday traffic. Either way, you are an adult now. Your preferences are valid. Some of us are fine at setting boundaries at school, but when it comes to our families, especially our parents, we fall back into unhealthy patterns. This can be especially true if your parents fell into the narcissist, controller, or guilt tripper categories.

Here are some helpful scripts.

. . .

Scenario: Your parents or extended family are upset that you don't want to visit them for the holidays.

Start by expressing your feelings: "I understand that we usually spend the holidays together, but I've been feeling overwhelmed and stressed lately, and I need some time to myself. I need to set a boundary and take care of myself."

Set a clear boundary: "I won't be joining you for the holidays this year. I know this may be difficult for you to understand, but it's important for me to prioritize my well-being and take some time for myself."

Offer an alternative: "I'm happy to celebrate with you at a different time or in a different way. Maybe we can plan a special outing or dinner together once the holidays are over."

Emphasize the importance of respect: "I hope you can respect my decision and my need to set this boundary. I don't want to hurt or disrespect anyone, but I need to prioritize taking care of myself."

Enforce the boundary: "I understand that you may have different plans and expectations, but I need to set this boundary for myself. I hope we can still have a positive and meaningful relationship, even if we're not together for the holidays."

. . .

Scenario: Someone close to you makes passive-aggressive comments about your chosen profession.

For example, if your family thinks you are somehow underachieving by being a teacher. I've had to deal with such comments as: "You had so much potential. Why are you just a teacher?"

You can say the following:

"I understand that you may feel like teaching is not a prestigious or high-paying career.

I feel being a teacher is meaningful and fulfilling, even when I complain that it's hard.

Education has the power to change lives and make a positive impact on the world. I'm proud to be a teacher.

Please respect that, just as I respect your chosen career path."

It's also important to set boundaries with family and friends who assume that just because it's summer break, you are available to help them with any errands or chores they need to be done.

. . .

"I understand you may feel like I have a lot of free time because I have summers off. However, being a teacher is demanding and requires a lot of hard work, extra unpaid hours, and dedication during the year.

Much of my summer is spent on professional development, preparing for the next school year, and taking care of personal and family responsibilities that have been neglected. I need to carve out some time for self-care and rest, and I need time to slow down without being over-scheduled.

We don't get paid for summer. Many teachers pick up extra jobs or tutoring over the summer to make ends meet. Please don't take it personally that I can't spend the summer helping you with your to-do list. It's well-earned recovery time for me."

This could be an excellent area to set boundaries with limits.

For example, "I can dedicate one entire afternoon to helping you clear out of the garage. Would Tuesday or Thursday be better?"

Here are a few more boundary scripts to help you with family and friends. They do not have to do with teaching per se. But if you are someone who feels that your natural giving nature gets taken advantage of, you could benefit from learning them.

. . .

IF PEOPLE ALWAYS RELY ON YOU TO ORGANIZE OR PARTICIPATE IN party planning or host social events, you can use the same script principles discussed for declining requests at school. The secret there was to have a student-focused reason for declining. That's because you rejected the request of someone you work for, and you get paid for teaching students. With committees or social events outside school, you will likely not be getting paid. And remember, you don't need to give an excuse or apologize.

HERE'S A REMINDER OF THE STEPS.

1. THANK THE PERSON FOR THINKING OF YOU OR INVITING YOU.

2. Buy some time - tell them you will check with your schedule, partner, other responsibilities, or whatever is appropriate.

3. Respond via text or email if you think you will cave under pressure.

4. Keep your response concise and friendly. No apology or reason is needed.

5. Suggest an alternative if possible.

6. Wish them the best of luck with the event.

7. Consider a boundary with limits if it's appropriate and you feel like it.

HERE'S A SCENARIO: SOMEONE ASKS YOU TO ORGANIZE A **retirement party (family reunion, whatever).**

. . .

First, buy yourself some time and tell them you will get back to them.

Then respond in writing.

"Hey there. Thanks so much for thinking of me with regard to the retirement party.

As it turns out, I have many things coming up, and I promised myself this year that I would not over-commit myself. I need to honor my promise to myself and my boundaries.

I could take on a lesser role, such as helping with decorations. Or, you could check with (name another person) to see if they have any ideas.

Best of luck with the event! I'm sure it will be great."

Scenario: People feeling entitled to borrow things (car, money etc.)

Beyond setting boundaries with our time and energy, there are also times with family and friends when we need to set limits around our physical belongings. It can be very awkward setting a boundary with a friend or family member who wants to borrow something that is important to you, or even worse, borrow your car (think of the liabilities!) or money.

. . .

Here are some tips and scripts.

First, people will be less likely to take your denial as a personal rejection if you say that you have a blanket policy about what they are asking about. Remember, "I" language. Your denial is about your policy, not whether or not you feel the person is irresponsible or untrustworthy.

"I have a blanket policy never to lend my car to anyone. Not just for liability reasons but because I'm not comfortable with it.

Please don't take my policy personally. Is there another way I can help you? Maybe give you a ride to public transportation or call you a ride-share service?"

The same strategy can be used with lending money.

"I have a blanket policy never to lend anyone money. I have found that lending money compromises relationships, and you are important to me.

Please don't take my policy personally. It's a rule I made for myself, and I need to honor it. Do you want to brainstorm other ways to get some money?"

. . .

Or with lending items that are important to you.

"I have a blanket policy: I never lend my sewing machine (or whatever) to anyone. I use it daily, and I'm very particular about how others treat my things, especially if they are important to me.

Please don't take it personally. It's just a boundary that I have decided for myself, and it's important to me that I maintain it."

You get the idea. You want to communicate that it's about the policy you have set for yourself, not about how responsible the person is.

You want to communicate in a firm but loving way so that people feel you are rejecting their requests, not that you are rejecting them.

And, of course, you will only be able to do this if you consistently apply your boundaries. There's no way that one friend will feel OK with you not lending them your car if they learn you just loaned it to someone else the previous week.

To summarize, there are many areas in your personal life where you likely need to set healthier boundaries. While simple boundary scripts can help, with more delicate situations where the relationship is important to you, a more gentle and collaborative can be less stressful and productive. Dr. Marshall Rosenberg's Non-Violent Communication framework is an excellent tool to consider.

PART IV

Covert Boundary Issues

9

Codependency, Over-Functioning and Oversharing

In this bonus section, I will explore what I consider to be covert boundary issues- tendencies that people have that are detrimental to their self-care and healthy relationships but that they may not be aware of as having a root in boundary setting.

THESE ISSUES GO BEYOND YOUR NATURAL OR CONDITIONED tendency to be a helper, pleaser, and avoid conflict. You may recognize some or all of these tendencies in your behavior. Maybe none of it applies; maybe all of it applies. You may be somewhere in the middle.

I AM NOT A THERAPIST, AND YOU PROBABLY DIDN'T BUY THIS BOOK to dig into childhood trauma. But shedding light and inviting you to reflect on these areas may be the missing piece in why you struggle with boundaries. If you feel these hit very close to home and want to explore them more, I encourage you to reach out to a professional in this area for extra support.

. . .

Mindset

Here's the mindset that is most helpful to adopt. The lack of ability to set healthy boundaries is not a personality flaw. In most cases, people falling into the categories below have learned these responses as coping mechanisms.

I won't go into depth, but I want to give you enough information to ponder and ask yourself if these areas might apply to you. If you feel that they do, let the acknowledgment **empower you**. With awareness comes choice. Once you are aware of an issue or tendency, you can take action to correct it.

There may be any number of reasons that you have subconsciously adopted these tendencies. Likely, they were not your fault. But you do owe it to yourself and others to learn better habits. And there will be no shame in seeking professional help in doing so if that is what you feel is appropriate.

Let's start with the simplest one.

Oversharing

This is the tendency to share more personal or emotional information than is warranted in a situation. Often, it is inappropriate in professional settings and can make other people uncomfortable, overwhelmed, or unsure of how to respond.

OVERSHARING IS ALSO PROBLEMATIC IN THAT IT CAN BLUR THE lines of professionalism and boundaries. If you overshare, it can be harder to set boundaries later with people who feel they have permission to intrude on your personal life in ways you don't appreciate. They may also start oversharing with you in a way that makes you uncomfortable. Once the lines have been crossed, a precedent has been set.

OTHER THAN REASONS FOR PROFESSIONALISM, IT'S NEVER A GOOD idea to overshare with people who are not trusted friends. You never know how discrete co-workers or parents are, and you don't want your private affairs to suddenly become the topic of gossip or speculation. Regrettably, not all people have pure intentions. I have seen several careers in education unravel because of political agendas where information shared in confidence or carelessly was used to reprimand, harass, and ultimately dismiss teachers. I like to operate on a mindset and worldview that people have good intentions. But being cautious about what you share is always a good policy.

PEOPLE OVERSHARE FOR SEVERAL REASONS. MAYBE THEY SEEK understanding, approval, or validation. They may have the desire to be seen as open and approachable. They may lack self-awareness or self-control, leading to the sharing of overly personal information without thinking. But for some people, it can be a maladaptive coping mechanism resulting from trauma or abuse.

One area where oversharing can be particularly problematic is in the classroom. Teachers must balance creating and maintaining connections with students and setting appropriate boundaries with how much personal information they share.

We know connecting with students and creating a classroom community are essential to learning. However, oversharing can create an unhealthy dynamic in the classroom where the lines of professionalism are blurred. This can lead to students being confused about other boundaries or feeling they can openly disrespect them.

Additionally, students may feel uncomfortable hearing about the teacher's personal experiences or emotions. Knowing how to respond or interact with the teacher in this situation can be challenging. It may be hard for students to view the teacher as an authority figure if they know too much about their personal lives and emotions.

Over-functioning

What if you are the teacher who takes on too much, not because you have a hard time saying no, but because you volunteer for a disproportionate amount of extra duties, committees, and responsibilities? You may need help with over-functioning.

Over-functioning refers to the tendency to take on too much responsibility for the well-being of others, often at the expense of your needs and well-being. This can involve going above and beyond what is expected or necessary to meet the needs of others, such as taking on more tasks or responsibilities than you can handle, sacrificing too much of your own time and energy, or ignoring your feelings and needs to focus on the needs of others.

SOMETIMES OVER-FUNCTIONING CAN BE RELATED TO A CONTROL OR perfectionism issue. This happens when you feel that you are the only person who can execute the task to the standards you want.

BEING OVERCOMMITTED AND OVERLY BUSY CAN ALSO BE A maladaptive coping mechanism. Some people tend to keep constantly moving so they don't have time to dwell on other issues or problems in their lives.

OVER-FUNCTIONING CAN CAUSE PROBLEMS IN THE CLASSROOM. IF A teacher gets too involved in taking on tasks and emotional responsibility for students, students may not gain the confidence and competence to take on these skills for themselves. Not only can there be an unhealthy respect for appropriate boundaries between students and the teacher, but students can become overly reliant on the teacher. Although well-intentioned on the teacher's part, It can be the breeding ground of learned helplessness for students.

AS WITH OTHER FAILURES TO SET LIMITS, PEOPLE MAY OVERfunction to seek validation. While people who over-function on campus may present as confident, organized, and having it all together, their patterns may have a root in insecurity and needing external validation.

The other problem with over-functioning is that it is neither sustainable nor helpful. Eventually, you risk becoming burned out, overwhelmed, and resentful. When other people become too reliant on you and everything you do, they don't learn the appropriate skills for themselves. You are training people to be dependent on you.

And this brings us to the last covert boundary issue - codependency.

Codependency

The term "codependency" was coined in the 1980s by psychologists and researchers working in the arena of addiction treatment.

The concept of codependency emerged as a way to describe the relationships that often develop between people struggling with addiction and those close to them, such as family members or partners.

These relationships are characterized by an unhealthy dynamic in which the addict is overly reliant on the other for their emotional or psychological well-being, and the carer becomes excessively responsible for the well-being of the addict.

This dynamic becomes harmful to both individuals involved in the relationship.

In a more general sense, codependency refers to any time someone is overly invested in the feelings of others or takes on the responsibility for the feelings of others. It's the idea that, "I'm only OK if you're OK."

A teacher can be codependent in several ways. Some possible examples include:

• Putting the needs of their students ahead of their own, to the point of neglecting their well-being or personal life.

• Having difficulty setting boundaries with their students, such as by being unable to say "no" when asked for extra help or by going above and beyond what is expected to meet their students' needs.

• Being overly invested in the success of their students to the point of becoming extremely involved in their personal lives or taking on more responsibility for their well-being than is appropriate.

• Neglecting their professional development or personal interests to focus on their students.

• Struggling to set limits with challenging or demanding students and feeling anxious or overwhelmed when faced with defiance or conflicts.

. . .

As you can see, these actions, while they may be well-intentioned and stem from a desire to be supportive or helpful, disrupt the power dynamic in a classroom.

Our goal is for students to gain confidence in their skills and problem-solving abilities and learn to regulate their emotions. To do so, we need to be comfortable with students having a "bad day" and experiencing consequences. We can only effectively do that if we are not overly invested in their feelings and results.

Like other boundary issues, codependency often has roots in wanting to be validated and needed and fearing rejection. It can be present in all types of relationships. It can be a maladaptive coping mechanism or simply a bad habit. Either way, it can be harmful to both parties, allowing neither to be a fully functioning person with their own needs, wants, emotions, and experiences.

Codependent people are unhealthily tethered, and the invisible line between them and another person is missing. The goal of mature and healthy individuals is to be connected but simultaneously separate from everyone else. It's to be authentic to yourself and your preferences and desires. This allows everyone to have their feelings, make their own decisions, and have their own needs without constantly trying to please others and meet their needs. The goal is to choose to meet other people's needs when we love them and want to care for them, not out of obligation or an unhealthy bond of codependency.

PART V

All the Good Stuff in One Place

Conclusion

Setting healthy boundaries is essential to being a successful and fulfilled teacher. By learning to set limits and prioritize your own needs, you can create a healthy work-life balance and avoid feelings of burnout and resentment. Setting boundaries is the ultimate act of self-care, and you need to take this challenge on if you want a more positive teaching experience and your career to be sustainable.

By setting clear boundaries with your students, you can establish a respectful and professional dynamic in the classroom and reduce classroom management issues. You can protect your time and energy by setting boundaries with colleagues, administrators, and parents. This benefits you and all of your relationships. You get to show up as your best self and share that version of yourself with those you love, inside and outside the classroom.

Remember, setting healthy boundaries is a skill that can be learned. Use the scripts to help you until you become comfortable using your own voice and terminology. Even if some people in your life may initially push back on you when you start to set

Conclusion

boundaries, be patient with them and yourself. Keep your "why" front of mind. Every time you say "no" to someone violating your boundaries, you say "yes" to healthier relationships.

That's the point. The ultimate goal of learning to set appropriate boundaries is to have healthy, productive, satisfying relationships. Not only a satisfying relationship with your career in education but, more importantly, a satisfying relationship with those most important to you.

I wish you every success. If I learned to do this, you can too!

I'm here to help every step of the way. Be sure to look in the Supplemental Materials for a preview of some of the worksheets available to you **free of charge in the Companion Workbook**. If you haven't download it yet, go to

www.gracestevens.com/boundariesworkbook

10

The Scripts All In One Place

Scripts for Saying "No" at School

How to buy yourself some time before you respond to a request:

> "Hey, thanks for thinking of me. Let me check my schedule and get back to you."

> "I have a policy: I don't take on any new commitments without a 24-hour consideration period. Let me give it some thought and get back to you."

Give a STUDENT-FOCUSED reason for declining:

> "As you may be aware, this is my first year in this particular grade assignment. I feel I owe it to my students to spend any additional time I have gaining

a firmer grasp of the required curriculum so that I can best support their academic success."

> "This year, I find myself in a challenging situation where many of my students struggle with the skills they need to succeed in this grade. I will be dedicating any extra time I have to develop and implement interventions that help remediate their academic deficiencies." (Note - extra credit if you can get as many educational buzzwords into your reason for declining).

> "As you may remember, we had a lot of turnover in this grade span this year, and I am now the senior member of the team. I am obliged to devote much of my extracurricular time to training the new teachers on specific lesson planning, data collection, assessments, and interventions that we use. I feel this area of responsibility should be my main focus to ensure the success of all students in this grade."

EMAIL TEMPLATE:

DEAR PRINCIPAL:

Thank you for your invitation to represent our school at the district-wide curriculum committee.

As it turns out, I am unable to participate this year.

You may remember that….(student-centered reason)

I am confident that many other qualified staff members can effectively represent our school and ensure that the committee is successful.

Respectfully,

[name]

REMEMBER THAT SETTING BOUNDARIES IS NOT ALWAYS A "yes/no" proposition. Often you can set a healthy boundary by saying "yes" with limitations. Refer to the appropriate sections of the book for specific examples.

Scripts for Co-Workers

Time Suckers

> "Hey, Susie, you know I love chatting with you. I have so much to do today, and I promised myself I would focus during my prep period. Let's set a timer for 5 minutes to catch up. Or how about we catch up at lunch on Wednesday?"

> "Is this something you need right now, or can we discuss it on Wednesday?"

If the answer is that it can't wait, I would set a specific time and timeframe to address the issue. For example,

> "I can dedicate 5 minutes of my prep period to show you."

Toxic Complainers

> "Gosh, that sounds hard. Listen, I need to get to a meeting/yard duty/the office, but I hope your day gets better!"

> "Goodness, it sounds like that student is challenging. That's so hard. I have to get going, but I hope tomorrow is better. Get some good rest tonight!"

Bossy Boots

> "I feel disrespected when I am interrupted and when my ideas are immediately dismissed. I have as much to offer as everyone else on this team. I need to feel heard and respected. If I continue to be interrupted, I will request for this meeting to be continued via email." or "If I continue to feel invalidated, I will request a member of HR or admin sit in our next meeting."

> "I feel my ideas are as valid as yours. We tried your way last time; let's try something new. What do you think?"

> "I feel offended and condescended to when you use such an authoritative tone. We're teammates, right? I know we spend all day working with students, but the "teacher voice" doesn't work for me."

INAPPROPRIATE JOKER

> "I don't find that joke funny. It's offensive and inappropriate for a work environment. Please don't tell that kind of joke here."

> "I think some of us are feeling uncomfortable with that joke/comment. It's unkind and inappropriate to single out groups of people who have been discriminated against in the past. Please don't make comments like that here."

> "I know you might not mean harm, but those comments/jokes could get you in hot water with HR."

> "I don't get it. Can you explain to me why that's funny?"

THE GOSSIP

> "I feel uncomfortable listening to gossip about our co-worker. Can we talk about something else?"

or

> "I prefer to focus on my work and not get involved in gossip. Can we please talk about something else?"

> "I'm happy to talk about work-related topics, but let's avoid discussing our co-workers in a negative way."

> "It's important to respect our co-workers and their privacy. Gossiping about them just doesn't sit well with me."

> "I understand that you may have a different perspective, but I need to set this boundary for myself. I don't want to continue this conversation about our co-worker."

> "That sounds hard. Have you tried talking to them directly?"

> "I'm uncomfortable talking about someone who isn't here to defend themselves. I have a policy of not

saying anything about a person behind their back that I wouldn't feel comfortable saying to their face."

Again, not very situation requires that you go "all in" with a boundary script. If someone is a first time offender, or they seem as if they are having a bad day, you can always start with, "Are you OK?" Or one of the other "gentler" examples I gave.

Scripts for Parents of Students

Scenario: the parent wants to meet without an appointment.

"I understand that you would like to discuss this right now.

As it turns out, I have a full schedule today. I would be happy to schedule a time to meet with you to give this matter the time and attention it needs and to ensure student confidentiality.

I have office hours available on Wednesday afternoon. If we need to talk before then, I will check my schedule and email you some options tomorrow morning. Or you could address the matter by email.

If you feel the matter is urgent or a safety concern, I encourage you to talk to the office.

I am committed to your child's success, and I'm confident we can work this out."

SCENARIO: THE PARENT WHO IS QUESTIONING A GRADE.

> "Thank you for bringing this to my attention.
>
> I understand that you are concerned about your child's grade. So am I!
>
> While grades are important, focusing on your child's effort and progress is also important.
>
> I have spent a lot of time providing constructive and detailed feedback to your child in class and have given them the time and opportunity to revise and improve their grade.
>
> Once you have discussed this with your child, let me know if you would like to schedule a quick phone call. We can discuss how we can work together to ensure your child gets all the support they need and that they are taking responsibility for their effort.
>
> Here are three 15-minute time slots that I have available this week."

SCENARIO: THE PARENT WHO WANTS LAST-MINUTE WORK OR A LAST-MINUTE INDEPENDENT STUDY.

> "Thanks for reaching out to me. That's great to learn you are going to Disneyland for a week. What a fun experience for you all!

Please refer to the school policy on requesting independent studies. As teachers have many responsibilities and packed schedules, the school has a policy that requires advance notice for additional work requests. I am unable to produce an independent study by tomorrow.

Please check with the office as to what they suggest your child does to complete the missing work on their return. In the meantime, here are some additional online resources your child can access.

I hope you have a great trip and make many precious memories."

SCENARIO: THE PARENT WHO WANTS INFORMATION SO THEY CAN CONFRONT ANOTHER STUDENT OR PARENT ABOUT BULLYING.

"Thank you for reaching out to me. As a teacher, it's my responsibility to create a safe and inclusive learning environment for all my students. I take all reports of bullying seriously and will address any concerns or incidents that come to my attention.

If your child has experienced or witnessed bullying, please encourage them to speak with me or with another trusted adult so that we can take appropriate action.

I am happy to work with your child to resolve this issue and to get administrators involved if the situation warrants this. The school has protocols in place and will communicate with the necessary students and parents.

Per school policy, I am unable to disclose personal information about other students or parents, and it's important to protect the privacy and confidentiality of all individuals involved.

If you have additional concerns, I encourage you to contact the office."

SCENARIO: THE PARENT WHO WANTS TO BE YOUR "FRIEND" ON SOCIAL MEDIA.

"Thank you for reaching out to me. I understand that you would like to connect with me on social media.

As a teacher, I need to maintain professional boundaries with my students and their parents. While I'm happy to communicate with you through email or other school-approved channels, I prefer to keep my personal life private and do not accept social media friend requests from parents.

Please don't take this personally, as this is a universal boundary I have set for myself after seeing some negative things happen to co-workers.

Of course, if you have any concerns or questions about your child's education, please don't hesitate to reach out to me through email or phone. You can also schedule a meeting with me through the school's scheduling system.

I am fully committed to student success and will always support them and you in a professional capacity."

SCENARIO: THE PARENT WHO IS BECOMING HOSTILE OR SAYS, "I'M A TAXPAYER; YOU WORK FOR ME!"

"I notice that you seem very upset. I understand that you may have strong feelings about your child's education, but it's not appropriate for you to speak to me in a hostile or aggressive manner.

I too am a taxpayer. Technically speaking, I work for a school district. If there are specific policies that you disagree with, I encourage you to participate in parent club and school board meetings. We are always in need of passionate individuals.

If you would like to discuss concerns about your child with me, I encourage you to schedule an appointment. I would be happy to talk with you when you (or we) have calmed down and can talk respectfully and professionally.

I am stepping away from this conversation until we can discuss this in an appropriate manner."

Scripts for Students

Scenario: A student is talking back to you in class.

> "I sense you are getting frustrated. It's okay to be frustrated, but it's not okay to talk to me disrespectfully. We will both step away from this conversation for a few minutes. At that time, if you are still disrespectful to me, (state your consequence)."
>
> "I sense you are overwhelmed/frustrated/ not in agreement with me (whatever the situation is). It's okay to be overwhelmed but it's not to talk to me in a disrespectful tone. I am stepping away, and we will continue this conversation during recess/lunch/after school."

Scenario: A student asks to connect with you on social media.

> "That's nice of you to ask. However, as your teacher, I need to maintain professional boundaries with students. I'm happy to communicate with you through email or other school-approved channels for academic purposes.
>
> Please don't take it personally. I value my privacy and have a policy of not accepting social media friend requests from students or parents."

SCENARIO: A STUDENT ASKING YOU OVERLY PERSONAL QUESTIONS.

> "I understand that you may be curious about my personal life, but respecting my boundaries is important. I only share what I feel is appropriate about my private life. I'm here to support you and your learning, and I'm happy to answer any questions you have about the course material or other academic topics."

SCRIPTS FOR FAMILY & FRIENDS

SCENARIO: YOUR FAMILY COMPLAINS ABOUT HOW MANY HOURS YOU WORK

> "I understand that I work many hours outside of my contract, and that impacts our family time and extra household duties that you need to take on.
>
> I feel extra stressed and guilty when you bring this up.
>
> Please know that teaching is very important to me, and I accept that it comes with extra responsibilities and commitments. I value our time together and am setting boundaries at work to make it a priority. Thanks for being patient. It means the world to me."

SCENARIO: YOUR PARENTS OR EXTENDED FAMILY ARE UPSET THAT YOU DON'T WANT TO VISIT THEM FOR THE HOLIDAYS.

> "I understand that we usually spend the holidays together, but I've been feeling overwhelmed and stressed lately, and I need some time to myself. I need to set a boundary and take care of myself."

> "I won't be joining you for the holidays this year. I know this may be difficult for you to understand, but it's important for me to prioritize my well-being and take some time for myself."

> "I'm happy to celebrate with you at a different time or in a different way. Maybe we can plan a special outing or dinner together once the holidays are over."

> "I hope you can respect my decision and my need to set this boundary. I don't want to hurt or disrespect anyone, but I need to prioritize taking care of myself."

> "I understand that you may have different plans and expectations, but I need to set this boundary for myself. I hope we can still have a positive and meaningful relationship, even if we're not together for the holidays."

Scenario: You are with your family, and they make passive-aggressive comments about your chosen profession.

"I understand that you may feel like teaching is not a prestigious or high-paying career.

I feel being a teacher is meaningful and fulfilling, even when I complain that it's hard.

Education has the power to change lives and make a positive impact on the world. I'm proud to be a teacher.

Please respect that, just as I respect your chosen career path."

Scenario: Your family and friends assume that because it's summer break, you can help them with any errands or chores they need to do.

"I understand you may feel like I have a lot of free time because I have summers off. However, being a teacher is demanding and requires hard work, extra unpaid hours, and dedication during the year.

Much of my summer is spent on professional development, preparing for the next school year, and taking care of personal and family responsibilities that have been neglected. I need to carve out some time for self-care and rest, and I need time to slow down without being over-scheduled.

We don't get paid for summer. Many teachers pick up extra jobs or tutoring over the summer to make ends meet. Please don't take it personally that I can't spend the summer helping you with your to-do list. It's well-earned recovery time for me."

SCENARIO: SOMEONE ASKS YOU TO ORGANIZE A RETIREMENT PARTY OR OTHER EVENT.

"Hey there. Thanks so much for reaching out to me about the retirement party.

As it turns out, I have many things coming up, and I promised myself that this year I would not over-commit to things. I need to honor my promise to myself and my boundaries.

I could take on a lesser role, such as helping with decorations. Or, you could check with (name another person) to see if they have any ideas.

Best of luck with the event! I'm sure it will be great."

SCENARIO: A FRIEND WANTS TO BORROW YOUR CAR.

"I have a blanket policy never to lend my car to anyone. Not just for liability reasons but because I'm not comfortable with it.

Please don't take my policy personally. Is there another way I can help you? Maybe give you a ride to public transportation or call you a ride-share service?"

SCENARIO: A FRIEND WANTS TO BORROW MONEY.

> "I have a blanket policy never to lend anyone money. I have found that lending money compromises relationships, and you are important to me.
>
> Please don't take my policy personally. It's a rule I made for myself, and I need to honor it. Do you want to brainstorm other ways to get some money?"

SCENARIO: A FRIEND WANTS TO BORROW SOMETHING YOU ARE NOT COMFORTABLE LOANING.

> "I have a blanket policy: I never lend my sewing machine (or whatever) to anyone. I use it daily, and I'm very particular about how others treat things that are important to me.
>
> Please don't take it personally. It's just a boundary that I have decided for myself, and it's important to me that I maintain it."

NON-VIOLENT COMMUNICATION FRAMEWORK

Remember the four step process:

. . .

1. OBSERVATION. Bring attention to the issue without criticism or judgment by simply stating, "I notice" or "When I hear you say"

2. State how it makes you feel, "I feel"

3. State your need, "Because I need"

4. Make the request, "Would you please?" and/or enlist their input on a solution, "How do you think we can resolve this?" "What do you think we could do so that both our needs are met?" (Hint: an excellent place to start might be a boundary with limitations)

LET'S LOOK AT AN EXAMPLE. Let's say it bothers you that your partner looks at their phone when you are eating dinner together.

INSTEAD OF MAKING THE CONVERSATION ABOUT THEIR BEHAVIOR where they are likely to feel attacked: "You are always on your stupid phone! That's so disrespectful!" You would start with the observation. For example,

> 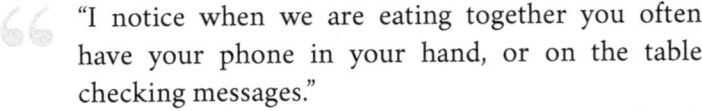 "I notice when we are eating together you often have your phone in your hand, or on the table checking messages."

NEXT, STATE HOW THIS MAKES YOU FEEL.

Beat Teacher Burnout with Better Boundaries

 "That makes me feel that you are distracted and I'm eating alone. I look forward to spending time with you and our conversations at the dinner table, and I need to feel that you are present with me."

THEN, MAKE A REQUEST.

 "How about we agree to leave our phones on the counter when we eat and not look at them or answer any calls until we've both finished eating and clearing up together?"

PART VI

Supplemental Materials

Remember to download the Companion Workbook. It has full-size PDFs to print and also additional exercises to help you on your journey. www.gracestevens.com/boundariesworkbook

What if you want to turbo-charge your boundary setting game?

There is an on-demand course with additional material, 25 + videos, additional exercises and a very cool diagnostic tool to help you see exactly where a lack of boundaries is causing you stress and overwhelm. For more information on this course, visit www.gracestevens.com/lifeback

Beat Teacher Burnout with Healthier Boundaries

Complete On-Demand Course

Beat Teacher Burnout with Better Boundaries

Yes/No Framework

By saying YES to this:

1.
2.
3.
4.

I'm saying NO to this:

1.
2.
3.
4.

By saying NO to this:

1.
2.
3.
4.

I'm saying YES to this:

1.
2.
3.
4.

Grace Stevens 2023

Extra Duties Inventory

Make a list of all of the "extra" duties that you are currently involved in that go above and beyond your contractual obligations. For each one answer the questions. This should give you a "snap shot" of your current commitments.

Type of Commitment	Stipend Y/N Amount	Scale 1-10 of your PASSION for this	Committed through the end of the year? Y/N

Take a realistic look at this snapshot. Be honest about whether the committees and activities add joy and satisfaction to your life or leave you feeling depleted and resentful.

Grace Stevens 2023

Beat Teacher Burnout with Better Boundaries

Declining "Professionally"

01 — Thank the person
02 — Buy yourself some time
03 — Decline without apology
04 — Give a reason that is STUDENT FOCUSED ← MAGIC PIECE
05 — Wish them luck/suggest alternatives

01 "Thank you for thinking of me."

02 "Let me give the matter some thought and get back to you."

03 "I am unable to take on this extra duty/committee at this time."

04 "As this year is a new grade assignment for me, I need to put all of my extra time and energy into understanding the curriculum to best meet the needs of my students."

05 "Best of luck with the committee/event."

Grace Stevens 2023

Non-Violent Communication*

*based on the work of Marshall Rosenberg

01 Compliment if possible
02 Observe - neutral fact
03 Describe Your Feelings
04 State Your Needs
05 Make a Request

01 "You know how I love chatting with you."

02 "When we start chatting we seem to lose track of time."

03 "I feel frustrated when I don't make maximum use of my prep period."

04 "It's important to me to be as productive as possible at work so that I can leave school at a reasonable hour."

05 "How about if we reserve all of our catching up for a Wednesday lunch date every week?"

© Grace Stevens LLC 2024

Good Teacher Karma

If you found the information in this book helpful, please consider recommending it to your colleagues who could also benefit from these strategies.

Also, **please leave a brief review** on whatever platform you used to purchase this book. It doesn't need to be a writing assignment! A few simple sentences about what you found helpful or who this book would be a good fit for would be great. Or even just smash those 5 stars ♡

Without reviews as "social proof," it's tough for books to find their way to their intended audience. As we know, many outstanding, talented educators leave teaching due to burnout and overwhelm. This information could help them and it would mean the world to me if you could help get the word out.

Finally, I am sending some positive energy your way. The world needs your gifts and your talents.

Thank you for all you do for other people's children.

About the Author

A former corporate girl, Grace quit VP life to pursue her dream job as a public school teacher. After 20 years in the classroom, she now focuses full-time on helping educators have a more positive teaching experience.

Grace combines her signature mantra, "Your energy teaches more than your lesson plans," with two decades of study in behavioral therapy, positive psychology, and NLP to create science-based habits for overwhelmed educators. She is the author of the best-selling *Positive Mindset Habits for Teachers* and host of the *Teacher Self-Care and Life Balance* podcast. 🎙

She is **the** Teacher Retention & Empowerment Coach for schools that want to stop the burnout cycle that causes their best teachers to leave.

For additional books, on-demand courses, podcast episodes, PD offerings and freebies visit: www.gracestevens.com

Also by Grace Stevens

Available on Amazon and all on-line retailers.

Check out Grace's podcast just for educators like you on Apple Podcasts, Spotify or any of your other favorite podcast platforms.

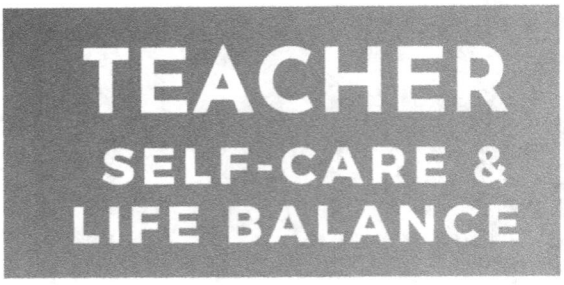

www.ingramcontent.com/pod-product-compliance
Lightning Source LLC
Chambersburg PA
CBHW050341010526
44119CB00049B/644